Survival to Revival: A Forty Day Journey Through the Wilderness

JOEL DE JESUS

True Potential
REACH THE WORLD

Revived And Kickin'

Survival to Revival: A Forty Day Journey Through the Wilderness

ISBN: (Paperback): 9781960024367

ISBN: (e-book): 9781960024374

True Potential, Inc.

PO Box 904, Travelers Rest, SC 29690

www.truepotentialmedia.com

Produced and Printed in the United States of America.

Contents

Introduction: Deserts and Storms

"Dear God,

Can you hear me? Are you there? I need you...

I am in trouble and don't know how to turn this around. Please, God, help me.

I can feel anxiety wrapping its claws around my neck as I am left gasping for air. I can't do this alone... I can't carry on. Why is this happening to me?

God, I beg you... please hear me... please help me find a way... do not abandon me. Do not let this be the end of me.

I need you. I am desperate for your intervention. Take this cup away; remove this yoke that is weighing me down. Please... please...lead me out of this wilderness. Just get me through this; help me survive."

I don't know why you picked up this book and why you are reading it. Perhaps a friend suggested it, or maybe something on the cover or title pulled at your heart. Maybe, just maybe, there is a God, and He has divinely planned that our paths and stories intersect at this specific moment in time.

I don't know where in the world you are or how the twists and turns have shaped your life. I don't know the dreams that you started with nor how far reality has tossed you in the opposite direction, much less do I know why the tears are running down your face and why your heart is heavy, but what I do know is that this prayer, or a similar version of this, resonates with you. At some point, we all have prayed or will pray this kind of prayer as we buckle at the sight of an unsurmountable mountain in our path.

Inevitably, somewhere along your journey through life, it will feel as if God has gone silent, and your problems have become so loud that they are all you can hear. At times like these, you are overcome and overwhelmed by your woes and are left gasping for air as you sink deeper and deeper into trouble. Looking back over the years, I have often prayed this opening prayer and pleaded with God that he show up and provide some reprieve. I have, at times, just needed a hiding place from the beating life was handing me. A quiet place, away from the strain. For you, this might be the prayer on your heart today as you fight to survive the storms or deserts bringing you to your knees.

So, I may never have met you, but I know you, and you know me. We are connected by this prayer, we are connected by our tears and our doubts, and we are connected by a God and Father who hears our prayer. I may not know much, but I know these two things.

Number 1. God loves you.

It is easy to forget this when we are in the middle of a storm or stranded in the desert, but never, ever let go of this truth,

> *For <u>God so loved</u> the world (that means you, reading this right now) that he gave his one and only Son (Jesus Christ), that whoever <u>believes</u> (puts all their hope and trust) in him <u>shall not perish</u> (or be destroyed) but have eternal life.* – John 3:16 (emphasis added)

If you remember nothing else in this book, just remember this: God really and truly loves you. His heart breaks for you when you cry out the desperate prayer that opens this book.

As a dad to two beautiful little girls, I know a father's love. Everything in me loves them but this is dwarfed in comparison to the love that God has for each of us. We can neither comprehend the width, nor the breadth, nor the depth of God's love even if we tried.

Number 2.... In this world, you <u>will</u> have trouble.

"I have told you these things so that in me you may have peace. In this world, you will have trouble. But take heart! I have overcome the world." – John 16:33 (NIV)

Jesus does not mince his words. I particularly like the New Living Translation's (NLT) wording, which puts it this way: *"Here on earth you <u>will</u> have many trials <u>and</u> sorrows."*

In short... You can expect trouble.

Neither of these points is a new insight or revelation. We have all heard this before, but we all too often seem to forget this. It has been watered down amid the battle in our minds. Ironically, it is precisely in these moments that we need to remind ourselves and cling to these truths. I will most certainly have trials and sorrows, but I know for sure that despite this, God still loves me.

Now, here is a question for you to ponder. Is the trouble that we are sure to have in this world all the same? Maybe when thinking about this verse, we need to distinguish between trials and sorrows. In this world, you will have deserts (prolonged trials) and storms (devastating sorrows). There is a difference, so when you are faced with trouble in the world, the first thing you need to determine is whether you are in a desert or a storm, a trial or a sorrow.

Storms are, of course, the sorrows that hit us out of nowhere. They are swift and crushing. They bring devastation and, in an instant, can leave our whole life hanging by a thread. The incomprehensible school shooting, the cold-blooded murder, the despicable physical violation, and the heart-breaking illness that young, innocent children sometimes must bear. The list goes on and on. Some may refer to these as the consequence of a broken and sinful world. But take heart that even in the storm, God is sovereign, and He remains in control even in the moment of greatest pain. Death, illness, and loss are storms that we will all face, but God promises that you do not have to face them alone and that you can take refuge in Him. He will shield and protect you; you will not be broken by this storm.

> *Yet when holy lovers of God cry out to Him with all their hearts, the Lord will hear them and come to rescue them from all their troubles. The Lord is close to all whose hearts are crushed by pain, and he is always ready to restore the repentant one. Even when bad things happen to the good and godly ones, the Lord will save them and not let them be defeated by what they face. God will be your bodyguard to protect you when trouble is near. Not one bone will be broken.* – Psalm 34:17-20 (TPT)

Read this Scripture again (No, seriously, do it now!). The storms and sorrows that we will encounter in this world are much like the natural storms and hurricanes we often see battering our coastlines. They come unannounced and swiftly pass by, leaving a trail of destruction behind them. All we can do is take refuge and wait for the storm to pass. We are then left to pick up the pieces and start rebuilding what has been destroyed. Jesus promises to be our refuge when the storms of life batter us, and He is your strength when you need to pick up the pieces of a broken heart and rebuild your life.

The other trouble that we can be sure to face in this world is the desert or wilderness. These are the trials that we face, and they differ from the storms in that God leads you into the desert so that you can be renewed in spirit and that your carnal ways can be put to death there. What is clear is that this is necessary for the old man to die and for the new you to be revived. In Luke 4:1, we read that after being baptized and filled with the Holy Spirit, Jesus left the Jordan and was *led by the Spirit into the wilderness*. The Old Testament also clearly shows how the wilderness is part of God's plan to sanctify his people before entering Canaan.

You need to understand that if you are currently in a desert, this is part of God's plan and purpose. The reason why you have been led into the desert is found in Deuteronomy 8:2:

> *...the Lord your God led you all the way in the wilderness these forty years, to humble and test you in order to know what was in your heart, whether or not you would keep His commands.*" – (NIV)

This verse is beautifully translated in The Message version as "*...God is pushing you to your limits, testing you so that he would know what you were made of.*"

The purpose of this book is to help you get through this desert, not just alive but revived. This is my hope that you do not just try and *survive* the wilderness but that you are *revived* while you are there. As with my prayer above, you, too, may be asking God to just help you get through the trials you're facing, but what if you are praying the wrong prayer? God does not want you to survive the desert; rather, His purpose for your desert season is that the old you die there and that you are made anew, that you find revival. He intends that you come through the desert not just saying that you are still *alive and kickin'* but in fact that you are now *revived and kickin'*.

We should also remind ourselves of God's promise in Romans 8:28, as we know that God causes everything, the storms and the deserts, to work together for the good of those who love Him and are called according to His purpose. However bad it is, if it is a storm that He has allowed or if it was part of his renewal plan for you, God will still use it for your good. Echoing the words of Joseph to his brothers in the book of Genesis, what they intended for harm, God intends it for good to save many lives.

Although I may touch on storms in this book, my main objective is to focus more in detail on the deserts that we have been led into. I want to look at the reasons why God leads us into the barren lands and why trials and hardship are part of a loving God's plan for you. While wandering through my own wilderness, God gave me forty images to illustrate the four phases we all need to go through to be revived in the desert.

- *Reflection – Why me and why this?*
- *Reaffirmation – What do you know for sure?*
- *Repentance – What's love got to do with it?*
- *Revival – Have you found what you're looking for?*

Even though the temptation may be to quickly read through and finish the book, I ask that you set aside the next forty days for this journey. Just as Jesus spent forty days in the wilderness and the Israelites had to endure forty years in the desert, I invite you to commit the next forty days as we dig deeper and reflect on why we have been led into this desert. We will then build our faith by reaffirming the promises of God and the truth that He is for us. We will discuss repentance as a consequence of love rather than of guilt or fear, and finally, we will prepare to recommit and fully surrender our lives to Him as we prepare our hearts for revival.

Note that the heart of this book is not to answer all the theological questions that arise when dealing with pain and suffering. I am not that smart. This book is just meant to be a real conversation from one seasoned wilderness wanderer to another weary traveler. I have purposely quoted Scripture from various translations to emphasis and highlight certain thoughts but would encourage you to read and study them in your own Bible version too.

So, over the next forty days, let's talk as we walk through the desert.

Part 1: Reflection

Why me and why this?

We will all experience trials in this world and will have to endure times in the desert. How we understand and approach this barren period in our lives is fundamental to our spiritual growth and the ultimate duration of our stay in the wilderness. There are a couple of basics that we need to grasp before we can proceed to reflect on the reason for this season...

Firstly, God has led you into this desert for a purpose. It is part of His plan; it is not a coincidence, and it is not misfortune. You are not a victim. In the book of James, it is written that we should "count it all joy" when we face these trials and are led into the desert as God is refining and purifying us.

Secondly, God is not punishing you for all your sins by leading you into the desert. When we are facing a testing period in our lives, and things are not going well, we are quick to presume that God is angry with us and, therefore, our circumstance is a punishment. You are not going to get out of the desert by being good or trying harder to be a better person. The purpose of the desert is not to punish you but to reveal what is in your heart. It is a process to show you what is within you and who is truly the king of your heart. It is a refining process that pushes you and encourages you to surrender fully to the Holy Spirit.

The first step to getting through the desert is to spend some time reflecting on why God has led you here. Over the next few chapters, we will consider what lies in the murky waters of your heart. Some of this you may already be very aware of, but some of it is so deep and will require you to be honest and truthful so you can bring it to the surface. The purpose of this process of reflection is not to condemn you but to shine the light into these dark corners of your heart.

My prayer is that you dare to do this and allow the Holy Spirit to show you what you need to leave behind in this desert. You cannot proceed into the Promised Land by carrying all this baggage, and if you are not willing to let it go, you may be stuck in the wilderness for a while longer. I know this is not what you want, so take my hand, and let's examine our hearts.

Day 1: **What's in a Profile Picture?**

Okay, okay... so to start, I have a confession to make. I am not big on the social media scene, but I have always believed in having an updated and complete LinkedIn account, as you never know which recruiters are viewing your profile and possibly considering you for that dream job. Although I have diligently kept all the information and data updated, my profile picture is a little outdated. When I say a little outdated, I mean that at the time of writing this, it was only taken fifteen years ago or 4 B.C. (that's Before Children). In fact, that picture is a cropped image of one of my wedding photos.

The reason I am still using this profile picture is simple, I like the picture and I think I look good in it, so why change it? As God placed this image of my profile picture on my heart, I wondered why I had never bothered to change it. Was it perhaps that in my mind's eye this is how I still saw myself? The handsome young man in that picture had not really changed that much in 15 years...or had I?

Come on, be kind. I just need to get a proper haircut, shave away the rough beard that is now highlighted with some silver streaks, and, yes, okay, drop a couple of pounds. Apart from these minor changes, I still look exactly like my profile pic... Right? No, not really. As I glance over at the image in the mirror, I am reminded of the toll that the last few years of wandering in the desert have taken on me. Does this sound familiar? If I am truly honest, the man in the mirror looks nothing like the man in my profile picture.

Maybe you have a more recent profile picture (airbrushed to perfection, of course, because you can), so you may think I am a loser. That is okay, but in truth, I am not really concerned about social media profile pictures. What is important is assessing how you view yourself in your mind's profile picture. Does it match the man or woman in the mirror?

A few years ago, I had a conversation with a work colleague, and he was telling me what a great athlete he was while in high school. As he kept talking, it became abundantly clear that he truly believed that nothing had changed, he was still this great athlete. He believed that he should still be the first name on the team sheet.

Now, I don't know how good he was during his younger days, but all I could judge was what I saw in front of me... and though I am no talent scout, I was having some serious issues reconciling his current shape with what he was communicating. In his mind's eye, he still saw himself as this athlete; it was the mental profile picture he had of himself. That is what he wanted to see himself as, and he was convinced that if he could lose a couple of pounds, he would be back to his best, but this was not reality.

Today, what I need you to ponder is your spiritual profile picture. Do you remember the time that you first came to know Jesus Christ as your savior? Do you remember that fire in your belly? I can still picture my younger self, and I was a bit of a Jesus freak. I would consume God's word constantly, and I was fearless about sharing Him. But is that still how I see myself?

If you were to question me today about my Christianity, I think I would sound a bit like my work colleague... I would go on about this time when I would be fearless in Christ. Recalling all my past victories and convincing myself that I am still this bold Christian. I may have gotten a little busy with life and kids and work and church, but I am still on fire for Christ...Right?

Well, not really... When I look in the mirror, I struggle to reconcile the spiritual man I see with my spiritual profile picture. It is almost as if the only thing left of that once all-consuming fire that raged within me is a few dying coals... What about you? Are you still on fire for Christ?

The real problem here is not the fact that we have backtracked but rather that we refuse to see that we have backtracked and are no longer alive for Christ. We only consider our "profile picture" or the mental image we have of our Christian Self, refusing to acknowledge the man in the mirror. We are still good people, we still go to church (most Sundays), we still read our Bible and pray (even if it is just in the car on the way to work) ... and God understands because He is a loving God. We just need to tweak a few things and move a couple of pieces around, and we will be back to our old selves, right? This is a lie. Christ needs to be the center of your life every day. Our lives need to be crucified on that Cross daily, and we need to let Christ live through us.

In the book of James (Chp1 v23-24), those who hear the word but do not listen are compared to those who see their image in the mirror but walk away and forget it. Is it time that you look in the spiritual mirror and see the truth? Are you REALLY still on fire, or are you just seeing an outdated profile picture? Someone once said you will only change the things you cannot tolerate.

When reflecting on our "profile picture," we need to look at the truth in the mirror and have an honest self-assessment of who we truly have become. Only once you are willing to see the truth and you refuse to tolerate it will you be ready to move forward and pass through the desert.

Reflection Question:

Who is the real you in the mirror, and why do you need to hold onto past victories or failures?

Day 2: **Your Not-so-Perfect 20/20 Vision**

Ummm.... Isn't 20/20 vision supposed to be perfect? I mean, isn't 20/20 like getting 100% for your eye test? Well, apparently not... 20/20 vision is actually not perfect, but rather, it's just normal good vision.

In simple terms, you would have 20/20 vision if, at 20 feet, you could read the same letters on the Snellen chart that someone with normal vision could read at that distance. You would have 20/30 vision if, at 20 feet, you could only read what someone with normal vision could read at 30 feet; therefore, your eyes are weaker than normal. Conversely, 20/10 vision would mean that at 20 feet, you could see what all normal folks would see at 10 feet. Would that mean your vision is more than "perfect"?

Furthermore, this standard Snellen chart eye test only measures the sharpness or visual acuity of your eyesight and does not measure or consider other factors like moving objects or colored objects. So, even if you had super 20/10 vision acuity, it probably still isn't perfect. But how does this all relate to your wilderness wandering?

What I am trying to show is that even though you may have a deep understanding of Scripture or have been gifted with spiritual discernment, it does not mean that you have a perfect vision of God's plan for you, nor does it mean that you can see your imperceptible weaknesses. Your spiritual vision may be great, but it sure isn't perfect.

I don't know how long you have been stuck in the wilderness nor why you can't seem to find your way out, but I would guess that it may have something to do with either what you cannot see *or* what you are unwilling to see. This imperfect vision may be what hinders you from navigating your way out of the desert.

It often is my experience, too, that wilderness prayers seem to go unheard, and God just seems to be silent, but this is just not true. God is, however, slow in responding because He can see what our "less than perfect" vision overlooks. He is not going to answer prayers just for the sake of answering them. We first need to address our "blind spots" and cure our "factory blindness."

> *The Lord is not slow in keeping His promise, as some understand slowness. Instead, He is patient with you, not wanting anyone to perish, but everyone to come to repentance.* – 2 Peter 3:9 (NLT)

This is exactly why He is patient in answering your plea in the desert. He can see what you cannot, and turning a blind eye to this leads to your peril. So, what do I mean by the "blind spots" and "factory blindness" that are keeping us desert-bound?

Blind Spots

Most of us got introduced to this term when we started learning how to drive. You can probably still hear your instructor shouting, "Check your blind spot!!!" every time you think of changing lanes, at least I do, but I had some narrow escapes that elevated my instructor's anxiety.

In truth, we all have these blind spots in our lives, too. Weaknesses and flaws in our nature that we simply cannot see but traits that are generally very easy to spot in someone else. Although some of these may always have been part of you, much of these may have unknowingly seeped into your character by the toxic jargon you have been feeding on. So, allow me to shake the tree.

What may have started out as just wanting to lose a few pounds and live a healthier lifestyle has unknowingly changed you on the inside, too. Regardless of what you profess in public, deep inside, you are now motivated by your vanity and what people think of you and your body. Fat burners, Hunger suppressants, whatever it takes to look good. You look at people differently, too, and are much more judgmental of their physical appearance. Check your blind spot!

Yes, I know you are not racist, but you can't see the stigmas around ethnicity, cultural background, or social standing that have developed in you over time. You prefer to live in neighborhoods and move in circles where most of the folk are just like you. They look like you, speak like you, and generally believe in the same things as you do. Check your blind spot!

Maybe you secretly delight when others stumble, fall, or are exposed. You do not know why you feel this way and would never admit it, but they have got exactly what they deserve, and that pleases you. Check your blind spot!

The list is endless and different for each of us. Pride, Greed, Jealousy, Bitterness, Anger, Success. God may choose not to move in your circumstances until these things come into the light because if they are left in your blind spot and not dealt with, they will grow and consume you. Check your blind spot! If you don't, you'll miss it, and you will perish.

Factory Blindness

Where blind spots are things we cannot see, "factory blindness," on the other hand, deals with issues we refuse to see. These are those things that we just do not want to deal with and rather choose to ignore. I was first introduced to the term "factory blindness" while working for a group of manufacturing companies. My boss coined this phrase to try and explain how factory staff gradually became blind to hazards or problems in their everyday environment. When such a potential hazard was initially identified, staff may have moved slowly to resolve it. After a couple of weeks of further procrastination and no decisive action, factory blindness would start setting in. Staff would walk by the problem daily but somehow could no longer see it or the dangers that had initially been flagged.

We also carry a hazard in us that we choose to ignore. Unconfessed sin. We convince ourselves that it is not that bad and that it is not harming anyone. We know that it is a problem, and we even confess that it is a sin, but we choose to kick the can down the road. As time passes, we fall prey to this "factory blindness." We become blind to the problem. By suppressing our conscience, we erode it. The initial disgust we had towards it slowly fades, and this unconfessed sin becomes a normal and acceptable part of our nature. Again, allow me to prod at you.

For you, this may be pornography or a sexual lust that burns in your heart. You know it is a problem, but you choose to conceal it and not bring it into the light. With time, it becomes bearable and tolerable, just a part of who you are. You convince yourself it's okay and harmless. Satan is hard at work at eroding your conscience and making this lust an acceptable part of your nature.

For others, maybe you have already acted on the lust. That business trip was more than just business. You have broken your vows, but you push the guilt away and justify your choices. Stop and listen to your excuses and justifications. It was just a physical thing with no emotions - I am just a guy, and all guys do this – As long as my husband doesn't know, it doesn't matter because I truly still love him - This is actually my wife's fault, she is not giving me what I need physically in this marriage. Lies, lies, lies... and we slowly start to believe them. By turning a blind eye to your failings and pushing them into a secret corner, you develop this factory blindness and can no longer see it for what it truly is.

The psalmist who wrote Psalm 119:29 was right on point here: *"Keep me from lying to myself, give me the privilege of knowing your instructions"* – NLT. Stop lying to yourself.

You may be struggling with addiction or substance abuse. Maybe your addiction is not to drugs or alcohol, so you are quick to glance over this, but do you have a bad case of "factory blindness"? The fact that you refuse to see your addictions does not mean that they are not there. Shopping or retail therapy... does this fill a void and make you happy? Social media, internet, video gaming, mobile phones... got you hooked? Maybe it's just food or sweet treats... Is this what is helping you cope? What about that sports team you follow...? And then work? Are you keeping yourself busy at work so that you don't need to deal with the other yucky stuff in your life? How important is the "win," and at what price?

When we come down with "factory blindness," we are no longer able to see these addictions and the hazards that come with them.

My prayer is that this chapter will not condemn you but rather that it will help you understand that Satan is seeking to destroy you. He deceives you and cons you into believing his lies, and then those lies become the truth that you swear by. If he can, he will place sin in your blind spot, where it can grow uninterrupted so that it can eventually take over you. He will also convince you to ignore or procrastinate on dealing with your known faults because he knows that over time, you will become desensitized to them and eventually become blind to them in your life. The devil's master plan is to slowly erode you.

It is time to shine Christ's light into these dark parts of your life. Don't worry about the consequences of bringing this into the light but rather about the consequences of keeping them in the dark.

Reflection Question:

What are you unable or unwilling to see in yourself?

Day 3: **Poker face**

The seven of hearts and two of clubs.... If you have played any poker before, you know that this hand is not the hand you are hoping for when you are low on chips and need to make a move. As you look down at this hand, your heart sinks, but you know...Poker face... Don't let anyone see your disappointment, keep a straight face, and don't give them a clue that you are in a world of trouble. If you show any vulnerability, it's over. You still have the decision to make whether you are going to risk it or not... But the most important thing is that you keep your poker face on before you make this decision.

When we hit rock bottom in life, we often feel the need to put on our poker face, but God wants us to think differently about failure, adversity, and vulnerability. In particular, we need to reflect on how we choose to deal with these setbacks. You see, God does not promise us "success" or "smooth sailing" when we decide to follow him; on the contrary, the opposite is probably true. Remember, the Bible says there WILL be trials and sorrows. However, the real question is rather how we will choose to deal with these.

But why trouble? Why does God let us suffer with trials and sorrows? The pious and spiritual answer is that God uses it to sanctify and purify our hearts so that we become more like him. That is true, but there isn't much consolation in that when it feels like I am lying on the floor and getting kicked about, I still have to put on a smiley face. But maybe there is more... perhaps God needs you to be real and vulnerable. What is your innate response to vulnerability?

God is truly not interested in your success but rather in your sanctification and salvation. Your eternal life is more important to Him than anything else. Your health and wealth are not that important when compared to eternal life. What does he need to do to get your attention? I think most of us can make peace with this, although we may still not be too enthusiastic about the specific trials he has chosen.

So, what are you going to do when these trials and failures hit? How are you going to deal with this bad hand that you have been dealt when you are already on the back foot? Do you put on your poker face? Conceal and hide it. I think many of us do this instinctively. Especially as Christians, when we fail or when we are weak, when we face a trial, our inherent wiring wants to cover it up and hide it from all those around us. Somehow, we convince ourselves that this failure or weakness is not "Christ-like," and we are ashamed.

One of our modern-day Christian fallacies is that once we get connected to a church, we will have "blessed" lives (I use that phrase very cautiously). We see everyone else in our congregation living this picture-perfect Instagram-worthy life, and we think this is how it always is once we sign on. We feel the need to always just pitch up for church, put a smile on our faces, and show everyone there just how "blessed" our family is. Everyone is happy, and everything is awesome, right? We are Christians and don't want to dwell on the negatives, right? God is good all the time, right? Whatever you do, don't show your weak hand; remember your poker face.

I believe that the first step in dealing with failures is being vulnerable and honest. We need to be transparent about the hand we have been dealt with. We need real Christians who are not afraid to expose their weaknesses and failures. I have always thought of life as a bit of a poker game. We get dealt a different hand at different times, and we keep these cards close to our chests. We bluff and play our way through the poker game of life. But what is our natural reaction to being dealt a bad hand? Are we open and honest about it? Are we naturally willing to share it with those we love and those whom God has placed in our lives, or does our pride hinder us from doing this?

There are several good reasons for the need to share your shortcomings and disappointments. Firstly, transparency kills pride. The two cannot co-exist. Pride lies to you and makes you believe that you can do it on your own. It wants you to believe that you are in control of your circumstances and destiny. If you leave pride unchecked, you will soon not need prayer, and you will soon not need God. Once you reveal your weak hand and admit your failings, pride is dealt a death blow.

Secondly, being transparent about our shortcomings allows those close to us to encourage and pray for us. It permits them to practice what Jesus commanded of them, that is, to love one another. Don't hinder them from the opportunity to grow their faith. Even more importantly, sharing our burdens allows them to draw encouragement and inspiration from the way we are dealing with this adversity. Please allow yourself to be loved. Galatians 6:2 calls us to share each other's burdens; this is a two-way street, and with good reason... when we are open and honest about our burdens and the difficulties we are facing, the devil loses his power and his hold over our situation.

Lastly, transparency allows us to give God His rightful glory. You see, this is how it works... If you reveal your cards, a seven of hearts and a two of clubs, move all-in, and the flop comes...seven...seven...two, all you can do is thank the dealer, right? If you are dealt an impossible hand in life and you have the courage to be transparent and show your vulnerability, if in this impossible trial, you can declare your faith and trust in God, what happens when you get your miracle? Who gets the glory? You can only lift your hands and give God the glory. And what about those who are witnesses to your faith in this trial? How will this shape and build their faith? If you had covered it up and hidden it away from them, how does that build their faith?

You see, God can change your circumstances and lead you out of this desert whenever he chooses, but what is the purpose of this wilderness wandering? Who is watching and observing how you choose to deal with adversity? How will your story impact their story? God has a purpose and good reason for your trial, and that might be to not only purify and sanctify you but also to lead others to Him. To achieve this, you need to have the courage to show your hand...and then trust in Him. I believe that if you can do this, it may be your first step out of the desert.

Reflection Question:

What are you determined to keep concealed, and why are you pretending to have it all together?

Day 4: **Traffic Blues**

Don't we all just love traffic? Not too long ago, I saw a meme regarding Atlanta traffic that made me chuckle. It had a picture of rush hour traffic at the I75/I85 connector, and the heading simply read, "Stop moving to Atlanta...We're Full." This seems very funny until you are the one stuck in that traffic trying to get to the airport to catch a flight. This stretch is often referred to as the land of the never-ending crash because they are consistently removing some wrecks from there. Now y'all know why Christian radio stations are so popular in the big ATL; we need all the help we can get to get through traffic.

So, what does one do when you are stuck in traffic? Finding another route is probably not viable as most of these are more than likely already backed up, and getting through that may even be worse. There is no way that you can go back. Yelling and screaming might make you feel better, but it isn't going to change anything too. Your only option is to just keep chipping away and crawling up the interstate.

While negotiating my way through this traffic, I got to thinking about how we deal with the traffic jams in our personal lives. When you get stuck spiritually in a rut, what do you do? There are no backroads to take and no easy way out of the hole. Swinging your fists and punching the air in anger at God is futile, too. Do you soldier on or rather set up camp in the middle of the highway? Rather than getting up each day and affecting the things we can influence and thus ensuring that we keep moving forward, many of us just give up, get comfortable, and decide to set up camp right there. When we find ourselves stuck in the desert, this may seem like the best option, but Scripture encourages us,

"Blessed is the one who perseveres under trial" – James 1:12

No matter how hard it is in this wilderness or how difficult the hardships that you must overcome are, remember that you are called to persevere through it and not remain in that barren place. Our reluctance to address and deal with the weight that God wants us to shed in the desert makes it easier to sometimes just accept our lot and start making a home for ourselves by getting comfortable in the desert. Imagine we took that same approach when stuck in peak-hour traffic: just switch off your engine, get out, set up your tent, and get comfortable on the highway.

The truth is, it is never nice to feel as if you are stuck, be that in a career you hate, a relationship that is dead, or a mid-life crisis. It is most certainly not nice to be stuck in an emotional black hole or a spiritual void, either. But no matter how stuck you are, you simply have to keep on moving. You cannot just resign yourself to the circumstances and convince yourself that you are better off remaining stationary.

This is especially true when we find ourselves stuck in spiritual traffic. Our faith seems dead and lacks substance. We may even be tempted to believe that this is the way it is meant to be. We get stuck in this "comfortable" Christian life where even though we are good and we attend church, we say our prayers and give our offerings; it all just seems to be going nowhere slowly. This is when we need to be reminded of our purpose, the end game.

As our lives gradually become centered around ourselves and our to-do lists, as they start revolving around our dreams and our desires, we lose focus on our real purpose, which is to

GO and make disciples of men. This is what we were made to do; we were all called to focus on His Kingdom and what is important to Him. We were all called to completely surrender our entire lives, all of our time, all of our possessions, and all of our dreams to Him. Our natural inclination is to push back against this, but spend enough time in the wilderness, and this will become clearer to you.

Once we take our eyes off Him and start looking at the things around us, we get stuck in traffic. We lose focus on the destination, and we come to a halt. We then start making this highway a home as it becomes too hard to keep on going because we don't know where we are going anymore. Soon, this intolerable traffic becomes bearable, and in time, it becomes comfortable. It has become so comfortable that we no longer want to move from this highway. This is our home, our comfort zone. But God wants us to keep seeking and driving towards His Kingdom; settling for a life on the highway is not the prize.

When you are in a spiritual comfort zone, you have a problem. You are stuck. God's purpose is for you to be His hands and feet and to go and do something for Him, but you are stuck, and soon you no longer want to move. One of the most tell-tale signs of being stuck spiritually is in our prayers.

When your prayers are more like a request list rather than a genuine, heartfelt daily surrender of self to His kingdom's cause, you can be sure that you are stuck in traffic.

"Prayer is not about asking. Prayer is putting oneself in the hands of God, at His disposition, and listening to His voice in the depth of our hearts." – Mother Theresa

You must grasp that God did not intend for prayer to be a tool you can use to twist His arm, but rather one that prepares and changes our hearts to seek and accept His will.

To get "unstuck," you need to start moving, and to start moving, you need to restart the engine. From a spiritual point of view, restarting your engine begins with your prayers. Aligning your prayers to seek and accept God's will and glorify His kingdom is a spiritual discipline that you must master; there simply is no shortcut or other instant remedy.

You need to find a quiet space, a closet or basement, for your prayer time. You need to literally get on your knees and audibly speak to God with words that come from your mouth, not just thoughts in your mind or heart. Remember, words are what carry power, not just thoughts. You should offer yourself to God, ask what He needs you to do, and listen for His direction. We need to surrender ourselves in prayer daily and once we follow this direction that He has placed in our hearts, then the wheels start turning again. That is when we start moving out of the wilderness.

Reflection Question:

What is stopping you from restarting your spiritual life and moving to where God needs you?

Day 5: **Braveheart**

Without a doubt, my absolute favorite movie of all time is Braveheart. Even though I am not of Scottish descent, every time I watch this, I am so ready to go to war with the English. The closing scene of the movie is enough to make a grown man cry. William Wallace has finally been captured and is being tortured. The executioner and the crowd plead with him to say just one word, Mercy, and in so doing, surrender to the English King, but he gathers his last strength and breath and instead shouts... FREEEEEEEEDDDOOOOOOOOM-MMMMM!!!!!!

Talking about freedom, let's consider our freedom in Christ. If the Son sets you free, you are free indeed (John 8.36). To state the obvious, freedom is the opposite of being captured or being a slave. To be truly set free or to be free indeed means that one is no longer captured or enslaved. But what are we slaves to? To a sinful nature, like pride or lust? What about being a slave to the law, to traditions, to religious ceremony? Maybe we are slaves to fear...a fear of full surrender and what it may cost us. Perhaps we have never even realized that we are enslaved and are just like the Jewish leaders who protested that they were not slaves when Jesus told them the truth would set them free.

Harriet Tubman was born into slavery in the 1800s and grew up under this bondage. Not only was she able to escape slavery and reach freedom, but she returned to save other slaves and help them to freedom. It is one of her quotes that sometimes keeps me up at night:

"I have freed a thousand slaves. I could have freed a thousand more, but they did not know that they were slaves." – Harriet Tubman

I think this is so true for so many of us Christians, too... we go through life believing we were born into "freedom" because we were born into a religion, and we never recognize that we are captive to our comforts, captive to our comfortable faith and captive to the fear of full surrender to God's will. We are unwilling to give up our religion to follow Christ. We are unwilling to give up our Christianity to truly follow Christ.

Like so many of you who grew up in a religious home, I had no choice but to learn to recite the Lord's Prayer by heart, but this line always caused me such great anxiety.... "Lead us not into temptation but deliver us from evil." I always had interpreted this "evil" that we needed deliverance from as some external evil force that was looking to attack us. It was as though we were vulnerable sheep, and this evil was the wolf waiting to pounce on us. I believed that "Deliver us from the evil one" was a plea for protection from this bad thing that was out to get us. Although this is not completely wrong, it is also not entirely true.

After attending a funeral recently where we recited the prayer in Portuguese, I found a new, deeper understanding of this line. In Portuguese, the line is *"livrai-nos do mal,"* which is more accurately translated as "liberate us from evil" or "free us from the evil one." This is quite different from delivering or saving us from the evil one. If I need to be liberated or freed, then I must already be captive to this evil one. This evil has already got me, and thus is already inside me and has already enslaved me and captured my heart.

I believe this evil that has us captive and which we need to be liberated from is anything that stops us from doing the will of

Christ and surrendering completely to His will. It has taken God's place in our hearts. Anything in us that stands in the way of what God's plan is. We need to be delivered from this so that we can live a life that is fully surrendered to Christ.

In Matthew 16:13, Jesus questions his disciples, "Who do the people say I am?" Hearing their answers, He then flips the question to them and asks them, "But what about you? Who do you say I am?" and Peter responds, "You are the Messiah, the Son of the living God." This may seem like a standard answer for us in today's world, but for Peter, a Jew, to say these words at this point in history was revolutionary and a huge statement of faith. Then, from verses 17 to 19, Jesus praises Peter for this faith and calls him blessed. Jesus refers to Peter as the Rock on which He will build the church, but Peter the Rock is about to go from hero to zero in 4 verses.

When Jesus starts to reveal to his disciples what His purpose is and that the will of God is for Him to be put to death, Peter calls Him aside and rebukes Him, saying that this will not happen. Peter is stepping forward and doing what he thinks is best by vowing to protect Jesus at all costs, even with his life. This seems pretty noble, and he has good intentions, but what he thinks is the right thing to do is against Christ's purpose. Jesus then responds to him, "Get behind me, Satan! You are a stumbling block to me; you do not have in mind the concerns of God but merely human concerns." Ouch!

Peter goes from being the rock on which the church is built to a stumbling block in 4 verses. Jesus thus calls out the evil (Satan) in Peter that Peter cannot see and that he is captive to, in other words, that thing inside Peter that puts self or the interests of self before God. We may have good intentions in all we do, but we fail to recognize that we are enslaved by the evil that wants to stop us from fully surrendering to Christ and doing what His will is.

So, what has us captive? From what evil do we need to be liberated?

Could it be the fear of losing everything, of having to give up our worldly comforts? Are we afraid that if we fully surrender, it means we could lose the security net that we have been saving? Will it mean that you must give up the basic comforts of your life? Pray that God delivers you from this evil. So many of us love Jesus, but sadly, our hearts love the comforts of these worldly things, too.

Could it be that we need to be liberated from the fear of being excluded and being left out in the cold? This fear of no longer being accepted in our community or family? Will we be labeled as Jesus freaks or people who deserted our roots to follow some crazy Jesus cult? Are we afraid that full surrender to Christ will mean that friends and family will not understand our decisions and thus push us to the side? Are you afraid of being alone, of being the only one swimming upstream? Pray that God liberates us from this evil. So many of us are good Christians, but our friends and family are just too important to lose.

Or maybe we need to be freed from the fear of serving others and getting our hands dirty? Are we willing to become emotionally, physically, and spiritually invested in the plight of others? The easiest thing to do is just write out a check to ease our guilt, but are we truly willing to pick up a broken person and love them? Are we afraid that full surrender means physically and emotionally becoming the hands and feet of Christ? Pray that God frees us from this evil. So many of us say the right words and even bring all our tithes and offerings, but we are afraid to love as Christ did.

Could it be that we are being motivated by the fear of failure? We spend our days investing our limited time in meaningless things in pursuit of what we believe will make us happy, but at what cost? Our intentions are good and noble, and we are doing our very best at winning the race, but never stop to realize we are actually running the wrong race. Our fear of failure pushes us forward and blinds us from seeing that the race we are running is in vain. Are you captive to this fear?

There are so many questions, but the answer is the same. We need to call out the evil in us, which is a stumbling block and hinders us from doing the will of Christ. You need to identify that you are a slave to it and then pray that Christ delivers you and liberates you from it. You may need to fall on your knees and shout...

FREEEEEEEEDDDOOOOOOOMMMMMM!!!!!!

These fears that enslave us need further reflection and consideration and therefore over the next few chapters we will dwell a little deeper into each of these and try to understand how they prohibit us from doing what Christ wants us to do.

Reflection Question:

What has you captive and what do you need to be liberated from?

Day 6: **Backup Plan? Check!**

I'm an accountant by profession, so I am by nature all for having a backup plan. In fact, for most things in my life, I have always had more than one backup plan. There was always a plan A, a plan B, a plan C, and a break-the-glass plan G (plan God). Part of my innate accountant temperament is to make plans and provisions for the future and to educate others to do the same. You need to make provisions today for future college fees, your retirement, etc. You also need to make provisions for or have a plan in place for when things go wrong...car insurance, life insurance, etc.

In the last chapter, we identified the fear of losing everything and having nothing as an evil within us that holds us captive and enslaves us. I would like to take a deeper look at this fear and what really lurks underneath it, in other words, what causes us to be enslaved by it.

Money. Let's talk about it.

Many of us Christians cringe when the topic of money comes up at church; we put up this wall because we believe that the church is after our paper (sadly, this is sometimes true, and if so, please find a new church). I think it is important for us to clarify two points before proceeding.

Number one, God does not need your paper. Understand that your tithe is not what God is waiting for to build His kingdom, but in the same breath, God does not want you to cling to your money and not use it to build His kingdom. God is not waiting to get something from you; He rather wants something for you, and only by learning to give can you receive it. God does not want 10% of what you earn; he wants 100% of everything you will ever have. You must surrender it all to Him and learn how to become a good steward or manager of His possessions and His assets that you have control over.

Number two, money is not just money. Money represents security. Money is a safety net for when the rug gets pulled from under your feet. This is why money is in constant competition with God. God does not have a problem with money, per se, but rather with the fact that we place our hope, our trust, and our faith in money and the perceived security that it promises. Money or our savings becomes our security; as long as we have some of it, everything is going to be okay. What we have saved is what is going to bail us out when trouble comes.

Many of us place our hope and faith in Christ only with our tongues, but sadly, our actions place our hope and faith in our savings accounts, our 401k retirement plans, and our insurance policies. Please don't misunderstand; I am not advocating that you should not have these because that would mean you are a bad steward of God's assets; what I am saying is that when your hope, your faith, and your trust migrate to these policies and accounts, then you're in trouble. God will not compete with these things for your hope and trust. You cannot have two masters; either you place your hope in the security that Christ offers, or you place your hope in the security that money and possessions offer you.

To explain this further, let's consider Jesus's very own in-house finance guy, Judas Iscariot. History has done a good job of casting Judas as the greedy and selfish disciple who betrayed and sold Jesus for 30 silver coins, and to this day, nobody wants to be a Judas. Think about how many Peters, Pauls, Marks, and Johns you know compared to the number of friends you have called Judas. Get my point....

However, Judas was the disciple who was trusted by Jesus to keep the communal kitty or cash bag. He was responsible for the group's money and for ensuring that they were responsible when spending it. What is important to realize is that Jesus saw him as the fittest of the twelve to do this job. So that alone says a lot about Judas, but something led him to betray Christ.

Many may argue that it was greed, but I argue that it was much deeper. I believe that the root cause was fear and his zeal to see Israel freed from the Romans. You see, Jesus had revealed to his disciples that he was going to die, that this journey they were on was going to end. Judas was no fool; he could hear the whispers of the religious folk plotting to get rid of Jesus. Judas was overcome with fear; he had become a slave to this fear. Was Jesus truly the Messiah that God had sent to liberate them from the Romans? What would he do when Jesus was no longer there? What was his backup plan? Judas was an accountant; he needed a backup plan or exit strategy, and he did what most sensible finance guys would do.

Already enslaved by fear of having nothing to fall back on, he started to make provision for when the wheels came off this Jesus train they were all on. We may not be able to identify with or relate to the greedy and selfish Judas, but I am sure we can relate to the Judas enslaved by fear and wanting to take matters into his own hands. We have all been there, and some of us are still there.

Are you afraid that your complete surrendering to Christ will cause you to lose everything and, more importantly, mean that you lose your security? Does having nothing and thus having no backup plans scare you? Is this fear holding you captive and causing you to go against what God wants in your life?

In Acts 5, we read about the story of Ananias and his wife, Sapphira. They decided to do what many new followers of the way were doing; they voluntarily sold their properties and brought the proceeds to the disciples to be distributed among the poor. It is important to note that this was a voluntary thing and that there was no expectation for new followers to do this, but many chose to. The problem for Ananias and Sapphira was that they secretly devised a plan to hold back some of the money and lie about the sale price.

Why would they do this? They must have wanted to keep something in reserve in case this whole Jesus thing ran out of steam. They were afraid of losing everything and ending up with nothing. Can we say they were greedy or selfish? No way, they would not have given anything if they were. They may have had good intentions, but they were unable to fully put their hope and faith in Christ; they needed a backup plan. And the best plan they could come up with was to lie to and deceive the apostles because they were captured by this fear. In the end, they both die that very day, and their clever plans to make provisions for the future appear to have been made in vain. This story ties up perfectly with the parable in Luke 12:16-21:

> *The ground of a certain rich man yielded an abundant harvest. He thought to himself, "What shall I do? I have no place to store my crops." Then he said, "This is what I'll do. I will tear down my barns and build bigger ones, and there, I will store my surplus grain. And I'll say to myself, 'You have plenty of grain laid up for many years. Take life easy; eat, drink and be merry.'" But God said to him, "You fool! This very night your life will be demanded from you. Then who will get what you have prepared for yourself?" This is how it will be with whoever stores up things for themselves but is not rich toward God.*

It is good to make plans and be responsible, but please be aware that God is not going to compete with your 401k plan or your savings account. Your hope, faith, and trust must remain pinned to Christ alone. Only then can you be truly liberated from the lies of Satan that have you captive and enslaved to this fear of losing everything and having nothing.

It is time to bury this fear in the desert; you cannot come out of the desert if you are still captured by this fear.

Reflection Question:

Is your backup plan exactly what is holding you back?

Day 7: The "GET OUT OF JAIL FREE" Card

One of the best chance cards to get while playing Monopoly is the "GET OUT OF JAIL FREE" card. It gives you a free out when you get yourself into a spot of bother. It sure would be great if we could whip out this card in the real world when we landed in trouble. Some of you more fortunate may have a great attorney's business card that would do the same trick, but, alas, that won't be free.

Continuing from our reflection on being captured by fear, I want us to think about being enslaved by the fear of serving others or of giving ourselves. Have you ever played the "Get out of serving others free" card?

We all know the parable of the Good Samaritan (Luke 10:25 - 37). A lawyer approaches Jesus and is looking for a loophole in the law: "Love your neighbor." Like any good lawyer, he focuses his questioning on the apparent grey area in this law, namely, who would legally be included under the umbrella of neighbor. In other words, at the absolute minimum, who is he legally required to love in order to still qualify for eternal life? Jesus's response not only seeks to define who is considered a neighbor but also interestingly goes on to define what it means to truly love this neighbor.

Jesus, the great storyteller, paints the picture of a man robbed during his travels and left for dead. This is no fault of the man himself, and thus, there should be no barrier to taking pity on the man and trying to help him. The characters who come across the man are not just random either; Jesus spreads the net as wide as possible. He chooses the best of the Jews, namely a priest and a Levite, and on the opposite side of the spectrum, the worst of the non-Jews, a Samaritan (from a nation of "half-breeds" who were generally hated by the Jews).

In our modern-day, that would be comparing our pastors, priests, senators, and mayors, people of high moral and social standing in our communities, to the worst of the illegal foreigners. The question Jesus poses is simple: which of these acted as a true neighbor? The ones of high moral and social standing who played the "Get out of serving others free" card or the outcast who was willing to get his hands dirty and serve? We need to consider this parable in context with everything that is broken in our society and local communities. Who is your neighbor, and how do you love them?

The Samaritan gets down and treats the man's wounds. He could have continued and then, upon arriving in the city, sent qualified people back to aid the man. He may even have donated to help with the costs. This would still have been a good and noble thing to do, but by getting down and helping the man, by showing him love and not just having sympathy for his situation, something beautiful happens. He becomes emotionally invested in this stranger's story. He is no longer a spectator or someone who just calls 911. He is not just praying for the man or donating to the go-fund-me account. The Samaritan becomes the hands and feet of Christ. The Samaritan brings Christ's tangible love to the broken man.

Jesus does not say what this act of love does for the wounded man; we can assume that he is grateful, but Jesus does say what it does for the Samaritan. It changes him; he is now emotionally invested. He doesn't just care for the man's wounds and leave him. He carries him to the city, takes care of his accommodation, feeds him, and when he finally must leave, instructs the innkeeper to take care of the man and that he will pay all these costs when he returns.

I guess this is exactly why so many of us are captive to the fear of helping or serving others. We are afraid of giving ourselves completely. We are afraid of becoming emotionally attached to this cause because if we do, we fear that it will consume us and that what we currently consider important, our families, jobs, and homes, will have to be moved to the back burner. It is easier to just write a check and, in so doing, end our obligation to love. We extinguish the guilt that is burning us. If we become emotionally attached, it means that we will need to give more of our time, more of our energy, more of our tears, and more of ourselves for this cause. And this frightens us. It frightens us so much that we refuse to do what Christ is calling us to do.

Many of us modern-day Christians are horrible at loving our neighbors. Firstly, in our definition of neighbor, we only include those who are like us. It is easy to bake a pie for Catherine who lives down the road and has just had a baby, but what about cooking a meal for the single mom Maria who lives in a rented room in the bad part of town?

Secondly, in our definition of love. We all carry two common "Get out of Jail FREE" cards, which automatically pardon us from having to love like Christ. The first card is the "I am going to donate" card; by playing this card, we convince ourselves that it absolves us from having to get our hands dirty. Are donations to charities important? Yes, of course, they are... but God still wants you to be his hands and feet, not because of what it does for the broken that you are helping but because of what it does for you.

The second card is the "I will be praying for you" card. This card is more often used in everyday life with friends and colleagues than with charitable organizations. We use this card because we truly do not want to get caught up in the cobwebs of other people's problems. We sympathize with their situation, we feel sorry for them, and we sometimes actually do remember to pray for them, but we really, truly don't want to get our hands dirty. We have other important things going on, and we are afraid that if we stop and love and care we could become emotionally invested in their mess. God wants you to pick up the phone, go for that cup of coffee, love, listen, and be that shoulder this person needs to cry on. God needs you to become invested in their story, not just for them but for yourself.

So, being liberated from this fear of giving of ourselves requires not just prayer but a step in faith. It does not mean that you need to go on a missionary trip to Africa. It simply means that there are areas in your local community where you can give of yourself and your time, not just your money; it means that you take that time and become the vessel that carries Christ's love to that person you know is facing a huge mountain. This is love.

James 2: 14 – 26 speaks about faith without works being dead faith. You cannot have faith without works. We know that good works cannot get you salvation, but good works are a direct result of this salvation. Good works are the product of us being saved, not a ticket to getting us saved. Giving of ourselves and our time, becoming emotionally invested in a cause, and being God's hands and feet are all a result of Christ's love for us and in us.

Please let us not play the "Get out of Jail Free" card to get out of doing good and loving our neighbors, but instead, let us surrender to the Spirit that is alive and working within us and go out and love.

Reflection Question:

Whom shall you love today?

Day 8: **Your Security Blanket**

We all have our favorite Peanuts character, for some of us, it is easy to relate to Charlie Brown and how he navigates his struggles with hope and determination or maybe it's Lucy with her bossy personality. If I had to choose, I would probably go for Linus who despite his evident strengths, still harbors these feelings of insecurity. He is super attached to his blanket and is terrified by the thought of being separated from it.

When we immigrated to the US, my eldest daughter, who was five at the time, developed a deep attachment to a stuffed toy rhino called Rhiney. My sister had given it to her at the airport as we were boarding our flight to the US, and he was not only a connection to her life in South Africa but also quickly became her security and protection in a brand-new world.

I believe many of us adults still have an emotional security blanket, even though we may not be aware of this. We cling to it and draw our confidence and security from it; we have a fear of letting it go or losing it. This emotional security blanket is our tribe, the people who we have around us. Our family, our friends, and our acquaintances. More specifically, many of us have a fear of being excluded from our circles and being left in the cold. Many of us are slaves to this fear, and it may prohibit us from doing what Christ wants us to do. When what people in our circles expect from us collides with what God has planned for us, we are faced with the fear of being pushed aside and treated differently. We are faced with the fear of being separated from our emotional security blanket.

Jesus knew that the emotional tie to our tribes and becoming captive to the fear of being cast away from our loved ones would cause many of us to freeze and not be able to fully surrender to His will. He says this in Matthew 10:35-39 and again here in Luke 14:25-27:

> *If anyone comes to me and does not hate his own father and mother and wife and children and brothers and sisters, yes, and even his own life, he cannot be my disciple. Whoever does not bear his own cross and come after me cannot be my disciple.*

Following Jesus and truly becoming his disciple means letting go of this security blanket that is our family and our circles. Of course, we still love our children and parents, but doing Christ's will and following his purpose now overtakes this love. Once we fully surrender to Christ, we are set free from the fear of being exiled and cast aside by those we love. Our choices are no longer defined by the expectations of our family and friends but rather by what Christ is calling us to do, even if it means being labeled or abandoned.

I grew up in a traditional Portuguese home and had many Greek and Italian friends while growing up. The one thing we had in common was that our traditional faith and churches were very much entrenched in our cultures. Church life and your faith were part of your identity. In other words, you couldn't truly be Greek if you were not Orthodox, and being Catholic was as much as being Italian as eating pasta. You could not separate your cultural heritage and identity from your faith and your church.

Once I accepted Jesus Christ as my savior, I was faced with a constant battle of choosing to do what God had put in my heart versus that which my family and church expected of me. The church's laws and traditions versus what was being revealed to me in God's word. For years, I found myself trying to balance these two magnetic pulls, but that failed miserably. In the end, to find true peace, you will need to choose... and your choice may mean you end up on the outside.

Eventually, for me, it meant having to leave my childhood faith. This inevitably led to me being pushed to the peripheral edges of my community and family. I was judged for going against tradition and religion and for choosing to do what Christ put in my heart. In truth, many see my current trials and struggles as a direct consequence of my choices but still, I count it all joy.

Even though we hate to admit it, we are just like most animals. We love to be part of a herd, a flock, a pack, or a tribe. We love to be included. When I reflect on the crucifixion of Christ, I am sometimes perplexed by the crowd that shouted, "Crucify Him." Was there really nobody among them with the courage to swim against the flow and plead Jesus' case? You see, in this crowd were the same people who merely five days earlier were throwing palms and their cloaks on the road to welcome Jesus, on the donkey, into the city of Jerusalem. We are just like the people in this crowd as we do whatever those around us are doing. We are slaves to this fear, and some of us never want to be freed.

I am not here to tell you to leave your childhood or family church; this may be exactly where God wants you. I am not here to tell you to leave your hometown or country where your roots are well established and your family is nearby. I am also not telling you to leave the career that you spent years studying for and working on. What I would like you to answer is why? Why are you staying? Is this what God truly wants for you, or is there some unwritten rule that society, family, or the church expects you to follow? Are you perhaps captive to the fear of being cast out or being excluded?

All I am asking is that you follow Christ wherever that may lead. Do whatever he puts in your heart without the fear of persecution, without the fear of being cast aside. Only then can you experience what it is like to be truly free. Let go of your security blanket and cling to the Cross. Turning to Jesus may mean turning your back on your family, but maybe...just maybe, they end up following you to Jesus. Perhaps they just might be waiting for you to break with tradition and lead them to the Cross.

Reflection Question:

Why?

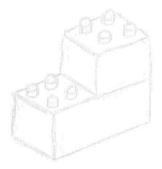

Day 9: **Everything is Awesome**

When the weather is miserable outside, there is no better way to spend some quality time with the kids than an afternoon of building your own LEGO land with all the odd and mixed blocks that have been collected from different sets. Fun for the kids, even more fun for dad... especially if this means you can get out of doing that long list of chores around the house.

The problem is what to do with these little creations once all the excitement of building them has vanished. The greatest challenge is trying to pack them away without demolishing them. Unfortunately, I had to learn this the hard way. Kiki, my eldest, was in tears for a couple of days and blamed me for destroying the entire world that she had painstakingly spent hours building. Dramatic.

Many of us spend our entire lives building our own little re-al-life LEGO world. We invest all our time, our energy, and our passion in laying down every little building block to create this perfect little world. We are little LEGO men running around in our perfect little world singing "Everything is awesome" but seemingly unaware and uninterested in the fact that our God can and will eventually decide that it is time to pack up the blocks. With a swift swipe of the hand, our entire self-built world comes crashing down. But why do we do this? If we know and believe that this is all temporary, why do we still invest all our time in being successful in this world? Is there something that is fueling this unquenchable drive for success? Are you perhaps captured by the fear of failure?

All of us experience this tangible fear of failure at some point, and it causes us to choose to follow one of two fatal avenues. We are either frozen stiff by this fear and end up doing nothing. The result is that we give up even before we begin and thus let the author of this fear win. Alternatively, we are driven to do too much in our own strength that may lead us to success, but what is the cost of this success?

I have always defaulted to the latter...always trying to do a little more and work a little longer to ensure that I did not fail. I could not bear the thought of failure, and I was driven by this fear of failure. As I wandered through my spiritual wilderness, I stumbled upon this quote, and it made me rethink my "success."

"Our greatest fear should not be of failure... but of succeeding at the things in life that don't really matter." – Francis Chan

Have you been fearing the wrong thing too? Is this possibly the reason that God has led you into the desert? Perhaps we should be reflecting on the things that really matter in this life instead of trying to win the wrong race.

At the end of chapter 10 in Luke's gospel, we are given an account of when Jesus visits the home of Martha and her sister, Mary. This seems a little out of place in this chapter as the entire chapter is dedicated to Jesus sending out the seventy-two followers to prepare the way for Him, and it also shares the parable of the Good Samaritan. But what is about to happen at Martha and Mary's home is as important for us as what precedes it in this chapter. Yes, it may be more important than Jesus sending us to share the gospel and also more important than us showing Christ's love like the Good Samaritan, but if we read too quickly, we may miss it altogether.

Martha invites Jesus and his disciples into her home, where she will feed and take care of them. Her sister Mary decides to sit at the feet of Jesus and just listen to Him, but Martha is distracted. She is super busy with all the preparations; she is getting dinner ready for all her guests and preparing the area for them to wash and a place for them to sleep. If you have ever had unexpected guests show up, you will know the pressure that Martha is under to make their stay comfortable.

Martha is doing good, and we all love the Marthas in our lives. They are the ones that slave in front of the oven for Christmas and Thanksgiving. Without them, there is no turkey, no baked ham. Without them, Christmas dinner would just be plain cereal or a toasted cheese sandwich. They are the ones who successfully micromanage every single small unseen detail of every family gathering and vacation.

Martha understandably gets frustrated and irritated as she is under immense pressure to get everything done. Annoyed, she approaches Jesus and requests that he tell Mary to get up and start helping with the preparations. Martha does not get the response that she is hoping for as Jesus says to her:

> *Martha, Martha, you are worried and upset about many things, but few things are needed—or indeed only one. Mary has chosen what is better, and it will not be taken away from her.*

What?? That is not fair on poor Martha!! She is busy breaking her back to make everyone comfortable, and Jesus takes the side of old lazy bones, Mary. You see, Martha was not doing anything wrong, but she was not doing what was the most important. She was not building a relationship with Jesus. She was so busy stacking block upon block in her LEGO land. She was so worried, distracted, and busy with things that were of less importance that she completely missed the purpose of Jesus' visit, which was to have a relationship with her.

This is exactly what we all so often do as well. We invite Jesus into our hearts but then get distracted by things that are not so important. We get busy with life and work, and kids, and church. Yes, all these are important, and we need to make time to get it all done but not at the cost of building a relationship with Jesus.

As you build your little LEGO world and as the fear of failure drives you to do more and work more and accumulate more and strive to be better with more success... please do not forget to stop and just sit at the feet of Jesus. Everything else is not that important. Believe me. Your job and your boss are not that important. Your clients and customers are not that important. Your church and friends...again, not that important. Your spouse and kids...yes, very important, but still not as important.

It is critical to understand that one of Satan's most effective ways of leading us astray is very often achieved by him stealing our time. He will deceive us into believing that the things occupying our time are more important than they actually are. He will strive to keep us busy, thus ensuring that our good intentions to one day spend more time with God remain just that: good intentions. As long as that one day is someday in the future and not today. When I think about my little LEGO world and how I get so caught up in it, this Bible verse comes to mind and forces me to stop and just go and sit at the feet of Christ.

"And what do you benefit if you gain the whole world but lose your own soul?" – Mark 8.36 (NLT)

If this verse doesn't keep you up at night, it should. Because whatever appears so important to us is, in fact, meaningless and worthless if the cost is our soul?

God desires that we nail this fear of failure to the Cross. It needs to be left in the desert. We are not to be driven by this fear, nor should we chase after things or be distracted by meaningless things. Every day, do what needs to be done, but make the time to come and sit at the feet of the guest that you have invited into your heart. If not, you may find yourself dwelling in the desert a little longer.

Reflection Question:

What is the real cost of your success?

Day 10: **Stuck on you**

Max Lucado has long been one of my favorite authors, and I can, without reservation, recommend any of his books. The advantage of being a parent was that I got to read his children's books to my kids, too, and quite often, the message pulled at my heart and spoke louder to me than its intended audience. Thank you, Max, for making the message so simple that even I got it.

One of our family's favorite bedtime stories over the years has been his book, *You Are Special*, which is a tale about Punchinello. For those of you without little ones, the story describes the lives of little wooden people who each have a box of stickers and go around the whole day sticking these stickers on each other. The good, talented, and beautiful ones get pretty golden stars stuck on them, while the not-so-perfect ones get grey dots. Punchinello cannot do anything right, and the harder he tries, the more he messes up. He ends up full of grey dots. In fact, he has so many grey dots that some people just walk up and stick a grey dot on him for no reason at all.

As he spends time with his maker, Eli, he learns that Eli does not see him as everyone does and he learns that the stickers only stick if you let them stick. We often let the way the world sees us define who we are. Their praises and tributes, their criticisms, and their disapproval. All of these stickers get stuck on us, and we allow them to stick, and it becomes hard to shake them off.

Maybe you have been led into the wilderness to get rid of some of the stickers that are stuck on you. You may have been branded as a failure, but God says you are not. You may think you are the bee's knees, but you are nothing without God. Our wise God knows that the desert is the perfect place for us to lose a few of these stickers, the ideal place to be humbled or built up, and the perfect setting to enable us to see ourselves the way Christ sees us, free of the world's labels.

Another thing that we are called to leave in the desert is our box of stickers. These stickers lead to division and prejudice. Think about your Democrat neighbor; has he got grey dots or golden stars from you? Does someone's political view influence our view of them? What are we sticking on our spouses, our friends, and our leaders? What if we are called to leave that box of stickers in the desert and choose to view people as Jesus does? Would that not make the commandment to love one another so much easier?

If we are honest, we will recognize our tendency to label ourselves and others, and to be influenced by these labels. We will also realize that we are in desperate need of shaking these labels off. To love as Jesus loves and to be able to do what Jesus would do, we first need to see as Jesus sees. No stickers.

In the gospel of John, we are introduced to a woman at Jacob's well in Samaria. Throughout history, she has been plastered with grey dots. Assumptions, prejudice, and ignorance have led many of us, me included, to judge her by how this text has been interpreted and how she has been portrayed. I am grateful to Eli Lizorkin-Eyzenberg for his insights and perspective regarding this woman at the well and her encounter with Jesus. After studying his work, I was able to see this woman as Jesus saw her and not as the world had labeled her.

The traditional or popular interpretation of this encounter presupposes the Samaritan woman to be of ill-repute and particularly immoral and promiscuous. The woman visits the well at midday in contrast to the custom of frequenting the well in the morning. This, together with the fact that she has had many husbands and is currently staying with someone who is not her husband, leads us to reach the irrefutable conclusion that she must have been an immoral woman seeking to avoid the morning crowds at the well. But the Scripture never says this. We choose to judge her by the grey dots that others have placed on her. Unfortunately, because of this prejudice, her entire conversation with Jesus is now viewed through this filter, and our understanding of the text is influenced by it.

With this starting point, the general interpretation is that as Jesus initiates a conversation with the woman, she ridicules his statements, and Jesus counters by exposing her sin. Convicted, she then raises doctrinal issues with him to avoid dealing with the real issues of faith. Once she realizes that he is not just a prophet but the Messiah, she rushes back to the village to tell everyone (yes, the same people she has been avoiding and who despise her for her promiscuous lifestyle choices), and they all believe her and rush back to meet Jesus. Needless to say, this version, however widely accepted, still leaves some open and unanswered questions. But what if we reconsidered the Samaritan woman? What if we removed the grey dots and started by seeing her as Jesus did?

Maybe she was not avoiding the crowds in the morning, maybe she was running late that day, or maybe the water she collected that morning had run out, and she went back to fetch more. Maybe she was well respected amongst the other women; she certainly appears to have a deep understanding of her faith and the differences with that of the Jews. Why else would they leave everything and follow her to Jesus?

What if the reason for her having five husbands had nothing to do with her choices but rather because she had lost them to illness and had been widowed, or maybe her husbands had been unfaithful, maybe she was unable to conceive and in terms of the law they chose to divorce her. Maybe the man she was living with was not a boyfriend but a relative who had taken this widow in and was caring for her as she would not be able to fend for herself. The truth is we do not know, but we have already tried, judged, and prosecuted her before understanding the cultural background of this society.

Jesus never tells the woman, "Go, and sin no more," or "Your sins are forgiven," as with the woman caught in adultery. When we read the story now, we can see that Jesus may not be exposing the woman's sin and reprimanding her but rather letting her know that he knows her past, he understands her pain and loss, and that this past does not disqualify her from a relationship with him.

This, in essence, aligns more with the Jesus we read about in the rest of the gospel. Maybe you are being falsely persecuted or judged unfairly. Perhaps you have all these grey dots stuck on you, and that is totally unjust. People don't understand you; they just don't know the real you, and they are so quick to pass judgment. Today, God is whispering to you...I know you. I know your past, and I know the truth.

As this chapter brings this first part of the book, Reflection, to an end, I invite you to pause and reflect on why God has led you into this wilderness. Clearly, we need to drop the box of stickers we have been carrying around. We need to love as Christ loves, and this is only possible when we see what he sees. Secondly, we need to grasp this truth today... Jesus knows you, and He knows the truth. Perhaps you are overcome by depression, and you are ready to give up. You tried, but nobody understood. You feel alone and misunderstood. Don't let the devil lie to you; don't let those suicidal thoughts take over. Jesus knows you; he knows the truth, and he feels your hurt and suffering. Please do not give up and throw your life away.

Just as he used the Samaritan woman's suffering to bring about salvation for her people, so her story speaks to your suffering and the plans God has to use you to save lives. Do not give up, don't you dare take your life... I am talking to you; take my hand, let me walk with you through this desert... I know it too well and the darkness and depression that it brings.

Reflection Question:

What lies are you believing about yourself?

Part 2: Reaffirmation

What do you know for sure?

As important as it is to reflect on the reasons why God has led us into the desert, it is even more important that this reflection not turn into self-condemnation. Many children of God get stuck in the desert for a lifetime as they are unable to go beyond this reflection phase. They keep looking at their very own failings and never look up to see God's grace.

The next step, or what I term "Reaffirmation," is the process of affirming who we believe our Savior is and what we believe his heart's desire is for us. It is the practice of defining the rock to which our faith is anchored, the truths on which we stand, and the reminder of the promises that He has given us. This is the step we need to take after coming to grips with our failings; it is the process of reaching out to grab God's outstretched hand. The book of Hebrews tells us to:

"Consider Him (Jesus) who endured such opposition from sinners, so that you (we who are also facing trials) will not grow weary and lose heart"- Hebrews 12:3 (NIV)

But what exactly does it mean to "Consider Jesus"? Well, we find this answer in the previous verse, Hebrews 12:2, where it says we should *"...fix our eyes on Jesus."* We should, therefore, fix our eyes on Jesus when we are in the wilderness so that we do not lose hope. In my darkest days, when I felt the weight crushing me, I kept feeling the following phrase pressed on my heart. *"It's what you KNOW when you are LOW"*.

In these low moments, my approach was to seek God's word for truths that I knew for sure that I could lean on. I needed to constantly reaffirm what I already knew about my Savior and His never-ending love and remind myself that He is faithful to keep His promises. During the times that you are at your lowest, you may be tempted to give up on your faith. But do not grow weary and lose heart because it is at this very time that you should be reaffirming the foundations of your faith.

• What do you really believe in?

• Who is this Jesus that you are putting all your hope in?

• What do you know for sure about God and his plan for you?

Defining and reaffirming what we know for sure when we hit the lows of the barren wilderness is the key to being revived in the desert and not just surviving through it. In these next few chapters, let's reaffirm what we know and are sure of.

Day 11: **Carved in Stone**

Literacy is one of the major differences between the worlds of the Bible and our own. People used to live in an oral culture where the spoken word was highly valued. In contrast, talk is cheap in this day and age, and everyone is ready to add their two cents. However, one thing that has generally stood the test of time is the written word. When words were committed to text, a great deal of thought and intention would go into it because it carried some sort of permanence as it was "in writing." Sadly, with the advent of social media, this is rapidly changing too. Every Tom, Dick, and Harry now have a toll to not just voice their silly opinion but publish it too...

Rewind a couple of centuries back, and with this understanding, one appreciates even more the weight of words carved into stone or wood. If papyrus was considered permanent, you'd better carefully consider what you wanted to put in stone or carve onto a wooden plaque. This is precisely why the Jewish religious leaders wanted to change the words that Pilate had written and placed on the Cross. Carving words in stone was concrete (Pardon the pun); you could no longer erase or burn it once it was set in stone. The Ten Commandments were cast in stone, and thus, the people knew there was no messing about, no arguing, no debating... That was the law!

In the next few chapters, we will commit to writing some concrete truths that we know for sure and that we need to reaffirm continuously in our wanderings. The first is this...

I know God hears me, and He will answer me.

You may be questioning how I am so sure of this...Well, for me, you guessed it, it was written in stone.

While struggling in my spiritual wilderness, I found myself pleading for answers and direction, but all too often, I doubted whether God heard these prayers. I think God's silence was the hardest part to accept. Just a simple yes or no, or even a maybe, is what we need, but the silence is what breaks us. In times like these, it is important to remember that God's silence does not imply His absence. Just because we are not receiving any answers does not mean that God does not hear us. I believe that God wanted to move in my situation, but he needed me to move out of the way first. Let's rewind to the beginning as I try to explain how I know, for sure, that God heard me and how He set the answer in stone.

As our eldest daughter approached school-going age, Brenda and I started flirting with the idea of immigrating to the United States. Like every parent, we have always wanted to give our children the best opportunities. As I prayed about this, I was convinced that this was God's plan for my family.

Well, I needed no further convincing... Like a bull in a china shop, I pushed to bring this vision to fruition. Such was the enthusiasm that Brenda dubbed me Captain America. I made all these plans, but God knew my heart. Unfortunately, in hindsight, I was probably blinded by my desire to move to America and proceeded to sugar-coat it as God's plan for my life. I know now that this was God's plan but not quite His timing.

So, armed with some very bad legal advice and this distorted vision of God's plan for my life, I pushed forward with my plans. Regrettably neglecting to bring my hidden selfish desires to the forefront, I forged ahead. I packed up my family and all we owned and headed to the US in pursuit of happiness. It did not take long for my American dreams to go up in smoke as the toxic concoction of this legal advice and my impatience to force God's hand yielded its devastating effects.

Not even two years later, after much adversity, I was unable to renew my visa and was forced to self-deport. So, there I was, back in South Africa, humbled. Gratefully, my sister-in-law took us into her home as we tried to pick up the pieces.

Being unemployed and having a lot of extra time on my hands, I started to wrestle with God. Why me? I was one of the good guys, but now I had lost almost all we had worked for. I had no income and no desire to get back to work, and we were thousands of miles away from our home without a prospect of ever going back. Come on, Jesus.... I know I may have been a little impatient, but did I really deserve all this as punishment? Was God not being a little heavy-handed in disciplining me? During this time, we applied on three separate occasions to return to the United States but were denied every time. Why had God taken us all the way to America and let us go through all that heartache only to bring us back?

As the weeks turned into months and as our prayers turned into desperation. I realized that even though I thought I was waiting on God for answers, the fact was He was waiting on me before He would move. I needed to fully surrender and follow His calling on my life, however inconvenient the timing was.

One night, as Brenda was praying specifically for God's direction, she felt led by the spirit to read Acts. By the time I had put the girls to bed and returned downstairs, she could no longer contain her joy as she felt that God had answered her through Scripture...

"Leave your country and your people,' God said, 'and go to the land that I will show you'" – Acts 7:3 (NIV)

Well, there it was in writing but that was exactly when I decided to go full-on Gideon and start seeking confirmation of God's answer. Was this really what God was saying or were we just seeing want we wanted to see again? I was not as convinced, but not to extinguish Brenda's enthusiasm I told her to write down the verse and that if this was truly what God wanted for us then He would confirm this Scripture through a different channel.

Over the next couple of months, things started to take a turn for the better as God opened an avenue for us to return to the US and for me to pursue studies in Theology. God had been faithful; he had heard our prayer and made a way out of the desert, but still, I had this seed of doubt deep within me. Was this God at work, or was I just bending His will to suit my plans and desires again? Did God really hear our prayer?

Before our planned return home, I spent a couple of weeks visiting my mother. As it happened, I ended up being there on Father's Day, and my mom asked if I would mind taking her to lay some flowers at my late father's grave. I had not been to my father's grave for several years. Through all my trials, I had often thought of my dad. Oh, how I wished he was still around; maybe he would be able to shed some light and offer some good advice. I couldn't help but feel as though I had let him down with the choices I had made and the way I had messed things up. But, as I lifted my head to place the flowers on the tombstone, I saw it...Carved in stone:

Genesis 12:1-2: *"The Lord said to Abram, 'Leave your country, your relatives, and your father's home and go to a land that I am going to show you.'"*

I mean, do you know how many verses there are in the Bible? How was this the verse engraved on my dad's tombstone and I didn't even know it? Confirmation of a verse and answer given to my wife. Coincidence? Not a chance! How is this even possible?

Let me tell you how it is possible.

1. God is real.
2. God hears our prayers.
3. God will answer us.

God heard all of my prayers, but He chose to remain silent as He waited for me to move out of the way so that He could do His thing.

> *Come and hear, all you who fear God; let me tell you what He has done for me. I cried out to Him with my mouth; His praise was on my tongue. If I had cherished sin in my heart, the Lord would not have listened;* <u>*but God has surely listened and has heard my prayer.*</u> *Praise be to God, who has not rejected my prayer or withheld His love from me!* – Psalm 66:16-20

As you pass through the wilderness, your faith will start to fade, but just because God is silent does not mean that He does not listen. God's silence does not mean He does not exist. You need to reaffirm this truth as you walk through your trials. Write this down and stick it on your fridge, your dashboard, and your computer screen. Don't let go of this truth, and remind yourself constantly:

God hears you, and He will answer you.

Day 12: I am no Superman

There are moments when I wish I could see myself the way my young daughters do. A few years back, they gave me a pretty cool Superman T-shirt for Christmas. You should have seen the delight and belief in their eyes as they handed me this gift. They genuinely were convinced that I was a superhero. Playing the role, I modeled my new T-shirt around the house, flying to their rescue and carrying them off to safety amid excited screeches. All this time, I couldn't help but think to myself... Bless them; soon, they will be wise enough to understand that I am no Superman. In all honesty, at that point in my life, I felt like anything but a superhero; I was a failure. Just a below-par accountant hoping to catch a break.

When you are barely surviving through a desert season, and you are grasping at the last strands of hope, the voices in your head become unbearably loud. Satan hijacks your thoughts and ramps up the accusations. There is no hiding from your mistakes, and the charge sheet is repeated until you break down. In your weakness, Satan seeks to destroy you with his lies and deception. The enemy we have in Satan and the spiritual battle that we face are very real. In these times, it is essential that you reaffirm the following truth...

I know God is my strength when I am weak. He will make a way!

As you are confronted by Satan's deceptive yet convincing rhetoric, you need to place all your trust in this truth: God is your strength and will make a way. God has got your back. You need to be certain that if you take refuge in him, he will provide all you need. One of my favorite quotes in times of trouble is,

"The will of God will not take you where the grace of God cannot sustain you." – Billy Graham

Think about that for a minute. It does not say the will of God will not lead you to difficult and testing times or that his will is to "bless" you with good fortune and success. Instead, it says that wherever God does lead you, He promises to take care of you, even in this wilderness. Even when you are on your knees with a crushed spirit, do not be afraid...Draw from Christ's strength and believe that God will make a way.

Growing up as one of five siblings, I very quickly had to learn to fend for myself. That, along with my innate pride and stubbornness, meant that I was always striving to overcome adversity by myself. I always made an effort to please everyone and attempted to solve my own problems without help. I had to be the one people could always rely on, someone who was tough and strong at all times. But alas, this perceived strength was, in truth, a weakness, and I would soon learn that I was no Superman.

In the summer of 2016, our family took a courageous step to seek a new life in a new country. For any of you who have done this before, you would agree that it is one of the most difficult transitions you can make. Not only are you in a new country where everything works a little differently but you have also been torn away from what you love and know. This was especially tough for my wife. Brenda had a very close relationship with her family, and immigrating to the US severed those close relationships. She was extremely unhappy, and I shouldered the blame. For the first time, our marriage was buckling under the pressures of resentment and blame, as well as an avalanche of problems, anxiety, and stress emanating from our move. But I convinced myself that I was tough enough to deal with it on my own, and so I did.

Shortly after our move, our eldest daughter started suffering from severe eczema, and it got extremely bad, quickly. We saw countless doctors, but it just got worse. It covered her entire body, and life in our home became unbearable. Bath time was a nightmare with a child screaming in agony; she could not stop scratching and would rip her flesh until it bled. Infections, new creams and ointments, steroids, antibiotics, and lots of bandages. I resorted to lying by her side at night, holding her hands to stop her from scratching as she slept, but to no avail. After little to no sleep, I would have to face a screaming wife upset that the child had managed to inflict such damage on herself overnight. But I soldiered on, keeping it together as best I could.

Instead of getting better, things seem to just get worse. I invested much of our savings into a new business as prescribed by our visa conditions. I failed to do the proper research and due diligence, which inevitably led to a calamitous domino effect. A failed business venture led to a failed visa renewal, which led to our legal status being revoked, which led to me losing my job, which would now mean self-deportation and financial ruin. I was no Superman; I was not tough enough, and this was just too hard.

I was weak, and Satan pounced by hijacking my thoughts. I wanted this all to end; our marriage was like a constant war of us screaming over each other. It no longer mattered that the kids were listening and watching as we hurled accusations and defenses across the room. This was not the happily ever after that I was promised. The truth is I was very unhappy and just wanted to end the marriage. Satan began his subtle lies about how it would just be better for everyone if we got a divorce. In my weakness, I flirted with the idea of giving up on my marriage or having an affair just to get out of it. But in my weakness, Jesus kept his promise and was my strength.

Not by my own powers to resist temptation nor my own self-control, but by God's grace was I able to steer clear of the destruction that lay ahead. But in averting this, I steered towards depression and suicidal thoughts. The weight was too heavy, and I just wanted to end it all. I did not want to live anymore. I had been sucked into this black hole of despair and depression. I couldn't see a way out; I just didn't want to do this anymore; life was too hard; God had forsaken me, and I no longer had anything to live for.

Satan went all in as his subtle whispers turned into roaring accusations. You are not good enough! You are the reason for everyone's unhappiness! There is no God, and if there was one, you would not be part of his plans! You are the cancer that is causing everyone pain; you need to do the right thing and get rid of the cancer! I was looking for a way out, wishing for a fatal accident or an easy way to end it all, and praying for an end.

In desperation, I lifted my eyes to the Lord; who was going to help me? I could not hold it all anymore...I was no Superman. I had been a Christian my whole life, said the prayers, sang the songs, and got the T-shirts, but here I was at Christ's feet with nothing. Just a failure with no hope of a comeback. As I cried for help, I heard God whisper, *"My grace is all you need. My power works best in your weakness."* – 2 Corinthians 12:9 (NLT)

I was weak, but I needed to trust that God was strong and able to deliver me. I was not going to do it on my own. I needed to take back my thoughts. An affair or suicide was not going to make anything better. At that moment, the world may have seen me as a failure, but two little girls still thought I was a superhero. How was ending it all going to make it better for them? Yes, I am no Superman, but I know a God who is way more than Superman.

All I needed to do was to stop listening to my highjacked thoughts and rather listen to and reaffirm the promises that

God had given me in his word, essentially that the Holy Spirit would help me in my weakness. So even though this is a hard chapter for me to write and share with you, I return to the verse above and echo Paul's words:

> *Three different times, I begged the Lord to take it away. Each time he said "My grace is all you need. My power works best is your weakness." So now I am glad to boast about my weaknesses, so that the power of Christ can work through me. That's why I take pleasure in my weaknesses, and in the insults, hardships, persecutions, and troubles that I suffer for Christ. For when I am weak, then I am strong.* – 2 Corinthians 12:8-10 (NLT)

You may be reaching the end of your rope in this wilderness. Maybe the only voice you are hearing in your head is Satan, and the options he is proposing seem like the only way out. Please do not give up; take shelter in Christ. Stop listening to the voices in your head and rather listen to the promises in your heart! Remember that this, too, shall pass. You will overcome. You will be revived if you can start by taking a small step and believing just this one truth:

God is your strength when you are weak, He will make a way!

Day 13: **Band-Aids for Brain Surgery**

In the introduction of this book, we briefly discussed deserts and storms. To refresh your memory, there is an important distinction to be made between the two as they relate to your spiritual life. Deserts are trials that God leads us to, and they are part of his plan to renew our spirit and bring us back to Him when we are separated from Him.

"God does not just sweep life away; instead, he devises ways to bring us back when we have been separated from him." – 2 Samuel 14:14 (NLT)

This book focuses on the desert and attempts to help navigate one through this spiritual desert, but there is still what I refer to in the introduction as storms. Storms are a consequence of a broken world and are meant to derail our efforts to return to God.

The bad news is that storms and deserts are not mutually exclusive. In other words, while you are battling through the desert and just trying to survive, you are not automatically given a pass from the storms of life. In contrast, you will probably soon find out that desert storms are almost inevitable, and there is a logical reason for this.

The devil will not just sit and watch on as you reconcile and work your way back to God. He is going to use every dirty trick in the book to fight for your soul. This is exactly his cue to muster up the major storms and send them your way. But despite this, you need to cling to and reaffirm the following truth:

I know God is my shelter in the storm; no weapon shall prosper.

The best encouragement I can give you is that even though the devil comes to kick you while you are on the ground, he will not prosper. You do not need to get up onto your feet to fight him; you only need to get up onto your knees. Also, take heart from the words of CS Lewis, "Affliction is often the thing which prepares an ordinary person for some sort of an extraordinary destiny." These storms prepare you for the extraordinary purpose and plan that God has for you.

In some of the previous chapters, I touched on my personal journey through the desert and how God had answered our prayers by walking us through it. Little did I know that this was only just the beginning of my journey and that there were still a few chapters left to write for this book.

When we arrived back in the US after fifteen very trying months, I could not contain my excitement. It was a new start, a new beginning; finally, I was pursuing my studies in theology and doing what I had always been called to do. What could possibly go wrong now? Well, Satan was not as enthused by my revival and was in no way ready to give up on me, too. I should have known that a storm was on the horizon, but I didn't see it coming. And boy, was this a major storm brewing.

The day after I had just commenced my theological studies, Brenda was responsible for two minor car collisions. She was unable to focus and was losing depth perception due to some severe migraines. We had always dismissed these migraines as nothing serious, but this time, they just didn't seem to abate. I dropped the girls off with a neighbor and drove Brenda to the ER that evening, thinking that we would be back for dinner with some strong medication and we could finally put these migraines behind us. They ran the standard scans and bloodwork, and we waited for the doctor to come and discharge us.

"Mr. de Jesus, your wife has a large brain tumor on her front left lob. She needs brain surgery urgently. I have just spoken to the surgeon and scheduled her for tomorrow morning...we will do our best. I am sorry..." WAIT! WHAT? How is this even possible? This cannot be happening! I mean, we have two little girls, God is for us, she is the healthiest person I know...They must be mistaken...How? Why?

Nothing can ever prepare you for a moment like this. I sank into the chair, and my soul screamed, "My God, My God! Why have you forsaken me? Why us? Why this? Why now?" A thousand questions but no answers... My faith was crumbling fast as I struggled to come to grips with what was happening. I was not ready to bring up our two little girls on my own.

"...Mr. de Jesus, do you have any questions?" the doctor asked. I had missed everything he said in between and glanced over at him blankly. I choked as I tried to speak, "I'm sorry, Doctor...I need to be honest with you. We have just got back to the States, and I have no insurance and no way of paying you..." as I finally broke down sobbing uncontrollably. That was it...Game over. Satan, you win; I was out. After calming me down and asking me a few more questions, the doctor put his arm around me and said another sentence that I would never forget, "Don't you worry about anything; we are going to take care of Brenda first, and we will take care of the rest later. We will work around the finances." The first Band-Aid.

The rest of the evening and morning was nothing but a blur for me as I tried to let the family back in South Africa know and process everything. By the time they rolled Brenda into the operating theater, we had mobilized a prayer army across several continents. The men in my small group dropped everything and were there with me. We waited as the time moved slowly, painstakingly. "You are not alone," I felt the spirit whisper in my heart. A second Band-Aid.

Thankfully, the surgery went perfectly, and soon, she was recovering in the ICU. As I sat at her bedside that evening, I felt the full force of Satan's lies and deceit overcome me. I could not talk to God that night; angry and feeling let down, my peace and gratitude quickly evaporated. This was not going to end well. I had to come to terms with the real possibility that I was going to be a single parent. Is this how God answers my prayers? As the evening went by, my anger turned to despondency and self-pity. God had no special plan or purpose for me. I was just an accountant and should go back to debits and credits; at least then, I could make enough to afford medical insurance.

The nurse taking care of Brenda could probably sense my heavy heart, and she soon prodded me with some questions. She shared her testimony about the trials she had to overcome and how God had remained faithful. Her son had tragically taken his own life. A boy who had served in the church youth ministry and helped many others through their suicidal thoughts. As she spoke, I was quickly convicted. Here, I had just witnessed the answered prayer over the brain surgery, but I was complaining and feeling sorry for myself. She, too, had many questions, but she only had one answer...Jesus. Another Band-Aid.

You see, Band-Aids don't take away the pain. They don't even heal the wound, but if you are the parent of a toddler, you know...Band-Aids are essential. Why? Because they provide comfort and consolation when you need it most. Over the coming weeks, I would receive many more Band-Aids. Little things that brought a lot of comfort, truthfully, if you had to ask me how I survived my wife's brain surgery...I would say with Band-Aids, perfectly timed by my Father in heaven.

Brenda and I had a rough time over the coming months; the biopsy results came back, and again, our world was shattered. The tumor was diagnosed as aggressive Grade IV Glioblastoma. Less than two years of life expectancy. As I struggled to deal with this reality, I was not the perfect and most supportive husband.

The devil has a master plan, a blueprint on exactly how to attack each of us. Don't be fooled; he is a mighty adversary. He won't give up; he wants your soul and will use all his powers to derail you. You must know this now before the storm comes. He knows your weaknesses and fears. He knows the areas of your life that you need to control, the areas to target that will shake your faith. For Brenda, it was her health. She had always lived healthy, making the best choices, and yet here she was with a brain tumor and a death sentence. For me, it was family and finances. My biggest fear of being a single parent and not having the means to provide was glaring me straight in the eye.

But if you know Brenda, you know she isn't going down without a fight, and she put it best when she said: "Satan chose to mess with the wrong girl." Truly, I can testify that what the enemy had meant for harm, God has turned for good, and I am reminded of Paul's words,

> *We are pressed on every side by troubles, but we are not crushed. We are perplexed but not driven to despair. We are hunted down but never abandoned by God. We get knocked down, but we are not destroyed... That is why we never give up. Though our bodies are dying, our spirits are being renewed every day. For our present troubles are small and won't last very long. Yet they produce for us a glory that vastly outweighs them and will last forever! So we don't look at the troubles we can see now; rather, we fix our gaze on things that cannot be seen. For the things we see now will soon be gone, but the things we cannot see will last forever. – 2* Corinthians 4:8,9 and 16-18 (NLT)

Maybe this verse is a Band-Aid that you need today. I do not know what the future holds or how this story ends. I do not know your story and the storm you face, but I know this, and I want you to remember this as you walk through the desert storm:

God is your shelter in the storm; no weapon shall prosper.

Day 14: **Hello?...Anybody Home?**

I am not sure how many of you will relate to this or agree with me, but I really dislike coming home to an empty house. I might just be too accustomed to being greeted by my crazy, beautiful life as I walk through the door. Kids running and screaming daddy, daddy. The smell of a delicious homemade dinner and music playing makes me feel like I am home. But if nobody's home when I arrive, I just feel so empty, so lonely. I just have this overwhelming sense of sadness when opening the door to silence. Hello?...Anybody home?

Now, this warm sense of homecoming quickly evaporates as, roughly two minutes later, I am ready for some me-time to unwind and relax. I know that might seem weird to some of you, but that's just me. The truth is, I hate arriving at any do or place and just seeing strangers. I immediately start scanning the room for someone I know, somebody that I can go and stand by. I admit it...I hate feeling alone.

As you wander through the desert, this lonely feeling is your one constant companion. You just can't shrug it off by finding someone to talk to. It is there when you wake up and when you go to sleep, right through every day. Even if you have people around you, you can't help but feel alone. The reason is that the spiritual wilderness is a place of isolation. You need this isolation to block out the noise of the world and to enable you to hear the spirit, but during this time, you need to be certain of the following promise:

I know I am not alone. God is with me; He will never leave me!

For some of us, this isolation and loneliness are very difficult to handle, especially if it continues over a protracted length of months or even years. Though God has designed this time for us to be still, Satan understands our unease and discomfort with solitude, and this gives him the perfect opportunity to attack. You can be sure that as Satan plotted to deceive Jesus as he was in the wilderness, so he will script a plan for you to fall. The first part of this plan is to lie about you being on your own. He begins by attempting to convince you that you are removed from God and outside his love. That you are not lost but have been abandoned, forsaken, and rejected. You are outside the net of God's love; that is why God has sent you into the desert. You are alone.

We do feel alone, and it is, therefore, easy for us to believe Satan's lies, but although God wants us to be still and step away into the desert for a while, he does not leave us alone. He is right there with you. Over and over in Scripture, God promises us this. Do not fear; I am near. Do not fear; I am with you. Do not be afraid; I will never leave you.

> *...and in the wilderness. There you saw how the Lord your God carried you, as a father carries his son, all the way you went until you reached this place.* – Deuteronomy 1:31

> *Do not be afraid, for I have ransomed you. I have called you by name; you are mine. When you go through deep waters, I will be with you. When you go through rivers of difficulty, you will not drown. When you walk through the fire of oppression, you will not be burned up; the flames will not consume you.* – Isaiah 43:1(b)-2 (NLT)

I am not just here to quote pretty verses from the Bible. I have been where you are now. I have felt so alone even though I was surrounded by people who loved me and cared about me. My smile covered a sea of doubt. How could God be with me and allow this heartache? I would much rather believe that he was not there; it was easier to reconcile and make sense of this than to explain a God of love who just stood there and watched my world falling apart.

Hello?...Hello?...Anybody home? God, where are you?

But the truth is God was not only there with me, but he was also carrying me as a loving father does, as the verse above promises. We are all no doubt very familiar with the poem, Footprints in the Sand. As we look back at the most difficult times of hardship in our lives, we will only see one set of footprints...We were not walking alone; God was carrying us.

I know that it is hard now, and my words may be offering you very little comfort as you question where God is, so maybe it is time for a theme song for this desert journey. Music has always been an important part of my life, as well as the worship of Christ, so it is no surprise that I found solace in praising and worshipping God when I was in the desert. I particularly recall a specific Sunday morning service when God, through the worship, said...Joel, you are not alone; I am with you.

Brenda had returned home after her craniotomy and was busy with her rigorous radiation treatment and chemotherapy. A couple of weeks had passed after the initial shock of discovering and removing the brain tumor. All of this started to weigh heavily as I grappled with the reality of what was now our new normal. I felt so alone as I withdrew into my own thoughts and doubts.

I attended church on my own that Sunday morning as Brenda and the girls stayed home. I remember that, as they started the praise and worship, I felt particularly downcast and burdened. I felt alone; I felt as if God had forsaken me. I was in church, but I was ready to give up on my faith. I felt God had given up on me, so I may as well just quit, too. But as the tears rolled down my cheeks, the worship team started singing a song that became one of my theme songs for my passage through the desert, *"Another in the Fire"* by Hillsong. As my soul shouted, Hello?...Anybody home? God answered... I am here in the fire with you; you are not alone!

I remembered the Old Testament story of Daniel's friends who were thrown into the fire and how the angel of the Lord came and stood in the fire with them. Now, maybe you are thinking that it is just a Bible story; it does not work that way in real life. I am here to tell you that that is exactly how it works in real life because as I stood in the fire, ready to give up, as the storm broke me and ripped the last bit of faith from my hands as I collapsed in the desert... God was there. He picked me up and carried me home.

As the months passed, God gave me another theme song, *"Wilderness"* by Anna Byrd. This song was a constant source of encouragement as I wandered in my wilderness, and it always kept reminding me that God was there with me. If this song is not currently on your playlist, you really need to get it now. It reminded me daily of God's promise that I needed to cling to when I was overwhelmed:

You are not alone. God is with you; He will never leave you!

Day 15: Faith on Crutches

If you have ever broken a leg or had knee surgery, you no doubt are forever grateful for the pair of crutches that helped you get around. Yeah, it may have taken a while to get accustomed to them, but once you got the hang of it, they were lifesavers. Without them, you would have been stuck and unable to get from place to place. Crutches offer us the support we need when we are unable to walk on our own; they give us the confidence to move about as we place our weight on them. But inevitably, the day comes when they have served their purpose, and they are stuffed into a storage closet until the next walking crisis arises.

Today, I want you to consider what it means to have "faith with crutches" versus having your "faith in or on those crutches," but first, we need to grasp and reaffirm the following truth before we can proceed:

I know God does not want me to dwell in this desert forever.

God has greater things planned for us, but we need to have faith in that plan. I think when you break it down, the difference comes in how you view those crutches. If you see them as an aid in your times of trouble, then that is all they can be for you. You break a leg and need something to help carry your weight. Crutches are the answer. Although you cling to these crutches, your faith is not in them but rather with them.

Your faith is still in yourself; the crutches are merely an aid to get you from A to B. As you get stronger, you discard the first crutch and hobble around with one, and soon after, you do not need it either.

For many of us, our faith in Christ is like this. Yes, we believe, we quote Scripture, we go to church, and we try our best not to commit any big sins, but we do not fully place our trust and faith in God. It is only when we are broken or have to navigate a crisis that we grab onto these godly crutches to help us get through it. Our prayer life becomes a little more intentional; we meditate on His word and believe a little more, but as soon as things get better, we put it back in the storage closet and go on our merry way again. It is almost as though our faith is only on standby just for when we need it. But what if God has a different plan for those crutches? What if God's plan for the crutches is to use them as stilts? Okay, I know that sounds a little crazy, but when I googled it, I found that this was actually a thing. There are crazy folk out there that flip their crutches over and turn them into walking stilts. Now, that is what I call putting your faith in the crutches. So much so that you are wholeheartedly committed to climbing onto these crutches turned stilts and risking an epic failure should you mistime a step or lose your balance.

The point is our faith is not merely as a comforter and helper in troubled times but as something that we can bank our entire lives on. God does not just want your faith to support you in crisis but rather to elevate you to your higher calling. So, what is this higher calling? What is God's plan for you, and can you fully place your trust in this plan?

As we have discussed, God has led you into this desert. He has allowed the trials. He has allowed Satan to test you. He has given you the crutches, or the faith, to initially support you as you wander in this desert but ultimately to elevate you to where He needs you to be. The choice, however, remains with you...Are you going to remain in the desert and grab hold of your faith only in trouble as a crutch to help you survive?

Or are you willing to see your faith as the same power that rose Jesus from the dead? Are you willing to flip your faith from crutches to stilts and stand on these stilts, placing your full confidence in their ability to lift you up high?

The Israelites experienced God's mighty miraculous power as he liberated them from captivity. They were comforted by his constant presence as he led them into the desert and provided for them, but as they stood at the foot of the Promised Land and the twelve spies returned with the dooming report of giants on the other side, they were faced with this choice. Were they going to trust and put their full confidence in God by standing on this faith and allowing it to elevate them to go and conquer the land, or were they going to doubt this faith and choose to only lean on it when being tested in the desert? Well, we all know how that ended; that generation spent the rest of their days in the desert.

For the most part, they still retained their faith, but they tended to drift from this faith as the desert got a little more tolerable, and they would lean on this faith when times got a little tougher. Their faith was just a crutch, and they could never see it as stilts. Their doubt and unbelief did not allow them to see the true power of this faith, and thus, they were not able to stand on this faith and leave the desert to go and conquer the Promised Land.

God's plan was never for them to dwell in the desert their whole lives and God's plan is, most definitely, not for you to dwell in this desert forever either. Yes, as we have discovered there is a purpose or reason for this season, but it is not forever. Peter confirms this in Scripture where he writes that we will endure trials just for a little while:

So be truly glad. There is wonderful joy ahead, even though you must endure many trials for a little while. These trials will show your faith is genuine. It is being tested as fire tests and purifies gold – though your faith is far more precious than mere gold. – 1 Peter 1:6-7a

You have a higher calling, but are you going to have the faith to turn your crutches into stilts and walk out of this desert, elevated and putting all your trust in Jesus? Or will you like many of those around you choose to keep wandering in this desert?

I have a dear friend who has been stuck in the desert for a long time. He is a wonderful man who continues to have faith through all his trials, but yet he remains in the desert. He has been in the desert so long that he has learned how to survive and get by. Although he truly loves Jesus, it seems that he has never been able to step into that faith and walk out of this desert on stilts to his purpose. I am grateful to him as he was there for me when I entered my spiritual desert. He quickly showed me the ropes and how to navigate my way through the desert. He taught me how to exercise daily spiritual disciplines of fasting and prayer. He motivated me to persevere in the trial, but as I prayed, I knew that this wilderness was not my permanent residence, and I had no intention of getting comfortable.

I realized very quickly that the only way out of this desert would be to walk out elevated on the stilts that God had given me and not just hang onto a crutch for support. I believe with all my heart that:

God does not want you to dwell in this desert forever.

Yes, God has led you into the desert, but you choose how long you will be dwelling in there with your crutches.

Day 16: **Still a race left to run**

As I held my worn-out pair of running shoes over the garbage bin, I had this crazy thought... I wondered what dreams and aspirations this pair of shoes may have had the day they left the factory. Okay, I am well aware that shoes do not have thoughts, but if this pair did, what would they have hoped for as they were shipped out to the shoe store? Did they dream of being the envy of all as they marched the first-team quarterback down the high school corridors? What were their thoughts now? As they dangled over that garbage bin, all busted and beaten up, was this how it ends? All those hopes and dreams...now literally hanging on a shoestring.

All of us also start our lives full of hopes and dreams, but very often, we end up in the desert, and these dreams quickly evaporate. It is exactly at these times that we need to cling to and reaffirm the following truth:

I know God is going to use my story for His glory.

The year is 1912 in Stockholm, Sweden, and on top of a garbage bin, there lies a mismatched pair of old shoes. They had been tossed away and were no longer needed or wanted by anyone. They had run their race, and this was the end of the road for them. At this point, a young man named Jim Thorpe was frantically looking for a pair of shoes. He was participating in the Olympics, and someone had stolen his shoes the previous night. He finds this mismatched, unwanted pair of shoes on top of this garbage bin, and by chance, they fit him. Jim Thorpe ends up winning two gold medals in the pentathlon and decathlon. Not bad for an unwanted, mismatched pair of junk shoes. Even though these shoes were written off, Jim Thorpe was still going to use them for his glory. (Well then, maybe there is still hope for my old pair of running shoes, too?)

This is exactly what God has in store for you. You may feel as if your story is a total wreck. The world has written you off, and you are defeated. You started with great intentions, you had big dreams, and you had an effervescent fountain of hope, but that all seems a very long time ago. Things are different now. You have been broken; you have been cast out into the desert. This Christian thing didn't quite work out for you, did it? Well, today, I am here to tell you that you are wrong. God is not done yet. You still have a race to run. He is going to use your story.

Life does not always turn out the way we planned, but that does not mean we should quit or give up. The first disciples of Jesus are often revered for their courage and belief in following Jesus, but was their choice truly that noble? When each of their lives intersected with Jesus, none of them were exactly living the high life. Most were fishermen who had to work very hard just to make ends meet; there was a tax collector who was despised by the whole community, some tradesmen, and some zealots who longed to incite people to rebel against Rome.

They all realized that Jesus was a great teacher, and when they decided to follow Him, there may have been a slightly selfish motive behind answering the call. They would all have had hopes and dreams of a better life being in the inner circle of a great new leader. They may have been motivated by the ambition of being the first followers and, thus, ultimately, of higher rank when Jesus rose to power. If Jesus was going to be the next king of Israel, being one of his main men was a much better prospect than being stuck on a fishing boat your whole life. I am sure that as Jesus' popularity amongst the crowds started to grow, they were probably feeling pretty good about their choice, but alas, this would soon change.

You see, following Jesus soon starts to become very difficult. Jesus' teaching is not exactly sitting well with the religious leaders, and they begin to publicly oppose him. Due to the disciple's association with Jesus, they are inevitably dragged into the crossfire. Those fishing boats are probably starting to look a lot more attractive now.

Well, we pick up the story in the Gospel of John at the end of chapter 6. Jesus is preaching what John describes as a "hard teaching" in the synagogue at Capernaum. He tells his followers that for them to truly live, they would need to eat his body and drink his blood. With our hindsight and understanding of the crucifixion and resurrection, this is much easier to comprehend, but can you imagine being in the room at that moment listening to this? No wonder Jesus started to "lose" the crowd, as we read below:

"From this time many of his disciples turned back and no longer followed him." John 6:66

Many of us may be tempted to abandon our faith when the teaching becomes too hard. Signing up for Christianity was supposed to make life better and easier, but truth be told, this desert is hard, and we are soon ready to turn back and head for the exit doors. The hopes, dreams, and aspirations we had when starting this journey have all evaporated, and we are left in a puddle of pain. If this is where you find yourself at this moment, then this next question is for you:

"'You do not want to leave too, do you?' Jesus asked." – John 6:67

This is the question that Jesus is asking us today. I, too, faced this question when my American dream had turned into a nightmare. Where was God in all of this? Why was He allowing all this to happen? As I sat in church one Sunday, I finally broke down...This was all too much. I felt like my race was run, and I was ready to abandon the faith, but what was the alternative... If not Jesus, then what was I going to anchor myself to?

Later that afternoon, while still considering this question, I got the following text message from my friend Chris, who had witnessed my meltdown at church:

> *Katie and I reflected on some stuff on the drive home, and I thought a lot today. I've got to say that watching you and Brenda go through all your trials over the last year and witnessing how faithful you guys have remained, I have been moved from the point of questioning and doubt to the point of being ready to fully surrender and to accept Jesus as my Lord and Savior. Thank you for everything you have shown me in this past year....*

Wow! Maybe my race was not done. Could God have used my trials and faith through these trials to ignite a spark in Chris? Was God using my story for His glory?

Maybe you started your journey just like that new pair of running shoes but have ended up on the garbage pile, all tattered and worn out by the hardships of life. Do not despair; do not lose hope. God still has a plan and purpose for your life. You still have a race to run.

When Peter, John, and James were faced with the question of whether to turn back to their fishing boats or continue to follow, they knew that they could not just rewind and go back. They had seen and experienced the truth. They had met their Messiah, and their hearts had been transformed.

I wish I could tell you that because of this choice, Peter and John got awarded lucrative book deals, a platinum record label and that they were blessed with a perfect family. I wish I could say that eventually, after the trials, they retired to their holiday homes on the island and had enough to live out the rest of their lives in comfort.

I think they knew that it was going to get even harder, but they believed that God would use their brokenness to build his church. Millions of people would share in the victory because they decided to persevere through the trials and not return to their fishing boats. They stuck around to run the race, even though all their hopes and dreams were no longer realistic prospects. I am reminded of Paul's words, which I hope will encourage you:

> *And what I'm going through has actually caused many believers to become even more courageous in the Lord and be bold and passionate to preach the word of God, all because of my chains.* – Philippians 1:14 (TPT)

So, what is your response? And what hangs in the balance of your choice? Are you heading back to Egypt, or will you persist through the desert? Do you still have a race in you that you must run? Do you believe:

God is going to use your story for His glory.

Day 17: **A Desert in Bloom?**

Has that heading got your attention? It surely got my attention when I first read it. We all know how Google algorithms recommend articles based on our search history, and it seems that while writing this book, Google believed that I was very interested in deserts. While scrolling through my feed, I found a news article about a desert near the Dead Sea that was in full bloom.

What? Is that even possible? I thought that the only thing that could grow in the desert was the odd cactus. I was wrong. It seems that occasionally, in years with extraordinarily high rainfall, it is actually possible for a barren desert to go into full bloom with a green covering and thousands of colored flowers. Wow, who would have thought that?

This article got me thinking. When we find ourselves in a spiritual desert, many things may seem impossible; it is at these times that we need to be reminded of the following truth:

I know with God, all things are possible even my impossible.

A desert in full bloom is our reminder that even though things may appear impossible in our current circumstances, we serve a God of the impossible who can do all things. Never be discouraged, and never lose hope. Impossible is nothing for God, as the prophet Isaiah emphasizes,

The desert and the parched land will be glad; the wilderness will rejoice and blossom. Like the crocus, it will burst into bloom; it will rejoice greatly and shout for joy... Then will the eyes of the blind be opened and the ears of the deaf unstopped. Then will the lame leap like a deer, and the mute tongue shout for joy. Water will gush forth in the wilderness and streams in the desert. The burning sand will become a pool, the thirsty ground bubbling springs. – Isaiah 35:1,2(a),5-7

Until at last the Spirit is poured out on us from heaven. Then the wilderness will become a fertile field, and the fertile field will yield bountiful crops. – Isaiah 32:15 (NLT)

There have been countless times in my life when God has shown up and done the impossible, as many of this book's chapters are testimony to. However, I decided that this may be the ideal time to reflect on how God took hearts of stone and a barren relationship and brought them into full bloom. Maybe this is where you are today. You want to forgive, and you want to move on, but it no longer seems possible. Your heart has turned to stone. Perhaps you are on the other side of a broken relationship; nothing you say or do can fix it.

My father had a really hard upbringing, and no doubt, it was probably what shaped him into the hard man he became. He was born and raised on a small island just after the end of the Second World War, and the repercussions of that war seemed to linger longer on the island as necessities remained in short supply for years. He lost his mother to cancer as a young boy and was forced to leave his home and family on the island in search of a better future. He headed for Africa, but life would not always go to script. Prejudice, racism, and unjust treatment by authorities were the standard treatment of any immigrant. In addition, he faced more trials, imprisonment, deportation, and being unfairly swindled out of the little he had. By the time marriage and five kids came along, my old man had become one tough nut.

It is difficult to write about my relationship with my dad. The truth is that for a very long time, I despised my father and vowed that I would never be like him. I know today that he intended no harm but just did not know how to parent differently. He did not know how to be affectionate and supportive. I think that he probably felt that the best way to keep us all in line was to be combative, aggressive, and by physically beating us, but considering his past, who could blame him? My childhood memories all pivot around that of an alcoholic father who found solace in the bottle and his friends and took out his frustrations by emotionally, verbally, and physically abusing those he loved. He could not control his wrath.

As I grew older, the rift between us only widened. I saw the world differently, and this made me resent him even more. We seemed to disagree on everything, from religion and faith to ethics, to family, to finance and business. Every conversation ended in an argument. There was no father-son relationship, and I didn't really care for one either. I was going to do things my way because his way sucked. We had moved too far apart to mend our relationship. Then came cancer.

One would think that this would change our hearts, and initially, it did as we both tried a little harder to be better, but as hard as he found it to love, I found it just as hard to be loved by him. I wanted to forget the past, but it seemed impossible. As he struggled with his health over the next seven years, we became tolerant of each other, but our bond had been severed too deeply, and we could never erase the past and leave it behind. For us, the father-son relationship we craved seemed a step too far. It was just no longer possible. He never asked for forgiveness, and I never felt the need to ask for forgiveness, either. I should have done more over these seven years. I should have made the time to drive him to the hospital for his chemo, and I should have asked him about his fears. I definitely should have listened and loved more, but I did not. Worse still was that through all this, I knew that I would someday regret it, but I was not able to love and be loved by him.

Impossible? That is exactly what I thought, but these seven years were not in vain. God was slowly working in our hearts, and he is a God who can make the desert bloom. My dad's health deteriorated again. His cancer had returned, and the years of alcohol abuse had left him with a severely compromised liver. The doctors told us to prepare for the worst as it was only a matter of time. My heart was heavy, not because of the prognosis but rather because I knew that my time had run out to turn my father to Christ.

On Wednesday, April 14th, 2010, we admitted my dad to the hospital. He had been in and out of the hospital over the last couple of months, and we all knew the drill, but somehow, this time, it felt different. That evening, as I lay in bed, my thoughts raced; if not me, then who? In a moment, my father's salvation became more important to me than going into the ministry and saving a thousand others. I made up my mind that as soon as the sun rose, I was heading to the hospital with the Bible in hand, and we were going to take care of business. I needed to be sure he was ready to meet his maker.

As morning broke, I called the office to excuse myself and headed straight to the hospital. Thursday morning became afternoon became evening...My father was under such heavy sedation that I could not say more than two sentences to him. He kept drifting in and out of full awareness. By Friday morning, I was desperate. Why had I left it so long? What had I been doing for the last seven years? Why had I stubbornly refused to love and be loved and allow for this relationship to heal? Surely, this was not the way this was going to end.

As I sat at my father's bedside in tears, ruing the countless missed opportunities to make things right, the local parish priest, Father John, walked in, and his timing seemed perfect as my father seemed more alert in the moment than at any point in the last two days. We spoke about the blood of Christ being the only way to the Father and how accepting, confessing, and believing in this makes one righteous before

God. That Friday morning, my father, as a 67-year-old man, accepted Jesus Christ, and all the angels in heaven rejoiced. God, in his wisdom, knew that Father John, a priest that my father revered and respected, needed to be there to affirm the salvation message I brought. What I thought was impossible, God had found a way to make it possible.

Over the next couple of days, my dad did not say much, but I spoke and poured my heart out at his bedside. I found forgiveness, and I was free to love and be loved. At least in my heart, the impossible had already happened; the desert was in full bloom. However, I was not alone in experiencing this. It was Sunday evening, and Brenda and I were with my dad. They had moved us into a private room as he continued to weaken. I was staring out the hospital window, and suddenly, I heard his frail voice call,

"Joel.... Joel...."

I rushed to his bedside, "Yes, Dad?"

"Joel... Do you forgive me?" he asked. I choked on my response as I broke into tears. Of course, I forgave him.

I had never heard my dad say sorry, let alone ask for forgiveness. My dad was ready to go home. A couple of days later, for a final time, he looked me in the eyes as if seeking reassurance to let go. I whispered to him the same words he had always used when asked how he was feeling,

"It's okay, everything's fine." Simple words for a simple man.

I bent over close to him and, with a quivering voice, said, "Rest in God's peace now...You no longer need to suffer. Jesus is waiting. It's okay, everything's fine."

He closed his eyes, took a few last breaths, and passed into the arms of Jesus. As I retell these moments that are forever etched into my memory, I am reminded that:

With God, all things are possible even your impossible.

So, my question to you today is this: What is your impossible? What is your hopeless situation? It may be a relationship or a circumstance, whatever it is...If you cling to it, it remains hopeless and impossible. Why not hand it over to God?

My Father, the man who took his first steps on that little island, who stepped on board a ship searching for hope, whose steps carried him to different continents and numerous countries, this man finally took his most important steps lying in a hospital bed.

We may spend many days in the desert looking for God, we may search for Him in beautiful cathedrals, we might try and find Him in the good deeds we do, and some of us try and find Him by reading the Bible from cover to cover. After all this searching, we are sure to know more about God, but we may still not have found him.

In my dad's last few days, he showed me where to find God. Where there is forgiveness, that is where God is.

Find forgiveness, and there you will also find God.

I hope you, too, can find forgiveness and, in so doing, see the desert in full bloom. It is not impossible.

With God, all things are possible even your impossible.

Day 18: Thirsty?

I am guessing that all this talk of the desert and wilderness must have you feeling thirsty right now, so please feel free to grab a cup of tea or a glass of water as we delve into this chapter.

We live in a world today where our thirst can be quenched at the snap of our fingers. Just walk over to the refrigerator or open the tap, and you can drink as much water as you like. For this reason, it is a little harder for us to truly relate to the experiences and understanding of the followers of Christ. For them, thirst was not simply just a memory of this one time after the ball game when all the vendors had run out of beverages, and you had to rush to the nearest drive-through for the up-sized Coke. Thirst was a daily reality. Even if they had water, it had to be rationed and used sparingly.

I am sure that the promise of living water, which would ensure they never thirst again, must have been desirable and must have immediately sparked their interest. Jesus uses this analogy to address a deeper spiritual thirst. Maybe for us today, it is harder to connect with this message, and we are led into a spiritual desert to truly experience what it is to thirst. It is at these times that we stand on the following truth:

I know God has all I need, all He needs is for me to trust it all to Him.

So, the question is, are you thirsty? I believe that as most of us are currently wandering through a spiritual desert, the answer is obvious. This thirst is why you are reading this book. However, the real question is, what exactly are you thirsting for? What are you praying for? What do you need from God? As you sip your tea, what is the unquenchable thirst in you?

The answer to this lies at the Cross. As you wander through the wilderness, the first oasis that you should seek is the Cross. It is exactly there that you will find what you are thirsting for. It is there that you will find this living water which will spring up, like a fountain, from within you and sustain you through the desert. Without this spring in you, you will continue to seek temporary relief and ration your water. Without the Cross, thirst will be your daily companion.

Before I get carried away in theology, let me try to explain my understanding of the relation between the Cross, living water, and thirst. The one thing that irks me about us as a modern church is how we tend to skip over the Cross and go straight to the empty tomb and the resurrection. We ignore Good Friday and go straight to Easter Sunday. The Cross is too gory and bloody, in contrast to Easter, which is joyous and filled with easter eggs and cute bunnies. Now, please do not misinterpret me. I am all for shouting "Christos Anesti" from the rooftop, but we miss so much if we do not pause at the Cross.

In some ways, the Cross is like the desert you are wandering in. It is unfair, unjust, and unpleasant, but it is necessary. As Jesus hangs on that tree, he is separated from God. For the first time in his life, he is unable to feel God's presence, hear God's voice, and experience God's comfort. As he takes all our sins on him, there is a great chasm between him and the Father. This thought just breaks my heart. I hear his desperate scream, "My God, my God, why have you forsaken me?" Those words haunt me as I sob.

What we need to understand here is that Jesus is not in anguish because of the wounds and pain of his physical body. He is not pleading with God to take away this pain or to end his physical suffering or trauma. No, the deeper and greater hurt he is experiencing is being alone and forsaken in his darkest hour. Does this even resonate with you?

In my darkest days, I have shouted these words too. Maybe this is exactly how you feel right now. You feel abandoned and forsaken in your desert. Where is God? Why has he forsaken you? Many times, when we find ourselves in the desert and we feel forsaken, we choose to unfollow God, or we pray that God takes away our suffering and that he brings an end to the pain. Jesus, however, is different. When God seems far from him, he does not lash out in anger nor demand justice or an explanation. No, instead, he utters three simple words... "I am thirsty."It is no coincidence that John seeks to highlight this phrase in his account of the crucifixion. John was there when Jesus promised "living water" to the woman at the well, water that would continuously quench her thirst. For John, water and the thirst for water carry a much deeper symbolic meaning.

> *On the last and greatest day of the festival, Jesus stood and said in a loud voice, 'Let anyone who is thirsty come to me and drink. Whoever believes in me, as Scripture has said, rivers of living water will flow from within them.'* – John 7:37-38

For me, the message that John is conveying is that in our trials and sufferings, when we feel abandoned in the desert, we should model our prayer on Jesus' words, "I am thirsty." In other words, our prayer should be to seek and ask for this living water that will sustain us through the desert. So, what is your prayer in the desert? Is your prayer "God, take this away, end this trial"? Are you looking to abandon your faith because you feel God has abandoned you? Or is your prayer rather, "God, I am thirsty for you; I am thirsty for more of you in me"?

You see, Jesus promises that he will put rivers of living water within you, but is this what you are thirsting for? Are you praying for this living water? Note that we are not talking about salvation here. The reason you may have been led into the desert is that you find a river of living water that will be placed within you and that will continuously be able to quench your thirst. God has all you need, and He wants to give it to you. What you need is living water, his Spirit, and to get this, all you need to do is say, "God, I am thirsty."

However, there is more; as Jesus nears his end on the Cross, he cries out... "Father, into your hands, I commend my Spirit." In his brokenness, he surrenders all of himself to God. He trusts all he is and all he has into the hands of His Father. Wow! What a wonderful example we are given on the Cross. In our darkest hour, not only should we thirst for more of God, but we should also surrender all of ourselves into God's hands. As we are filled with rivers of this living water that flows from within us and that quenches our thirst, we are able to fully surrender our lives, our trials, and our circumstances over to God.

As the dark clouds rise above you, as your enemies surround you, and as you walk through the valleys and wander through the wilderness, you need to stand on the following two truths,

- God has everything you need and all you are yearning for, and

- The only thing that He needs from you is complete surrender.

God has all we need in the form of living water, and he desires to give it to us, but He also wants us to surrender it all to Him, to commend our Spirit to Him. Once we have received his living water and have freely surrendered all of ourselves to him, then and only then, is He able to use us for His purpose. Then and only then, can we overcome the sin that keeps tripping us up.

So, are you thirsty? Are you going to continue to run to the temporary wells to sustain yourself?

God has all you need; all He needs is for you to trust it all to Him.

Day 19: **No Comebacks**

Brenda and I have always been very intentional about telling our girls how much we love them. Both of us were raised in households that did not particularly encourage verbally expressing one's emotions, particularly those of affection. I suppose it wasn't prioritized in general and wasn't the societal norm at the time. We were determined to raise our children differently and ensure that we all felt comfortable in expressing our feelings. However, looking back, maybe we overcorrected just a tad.

A simple "I love you" soon progressed into a sequence of one-upping each other. Neither we nor our girls were willing to back down, as each of us was certain that our love was greater. "I love you more," "I love you 100 times more", "I love you to the moon and back," "I love you that times infinity." This would literally go on and on and on for several minutes as we worked our way through all the ways we loved each other more. I am not sure exactly when it started or where she picked it up, but our youngest, Giana, soon grew weary of this constant back and forth, so she initiated the "no comeback" line. Whenever Brenda or I would tell her that we love her, she would simply respond, "I love you more...no comebacks," and that was the end of that.

Today's message is simple:

I know God loves me more...no comebacks!

Scripture says that were every man a scribe, and the entire world a scroll, and all the oceans ink still we could not pen or write God's love. Thus, I am under no illusion of the impossible task of trying to illustrate how great God's love is for you. All I can say is...God loves you more; no comebacks.

This reminds me of something I once read about a young parish priest who wanted to give a great sermon on God's amazing love. He prepared for weeks, diligently studying the work of great theologians and countless books on the topic. He was determined to ensure his homily would leave a lasting impression and have a meaningful impact.

That Sunday evening, he switched off the lights in the church and lit a small candle. He did not say a single word but just watched as the candle burned. It only generated enough light to illuminate his face. He then walked over to the large cross behind the altar carrying this small candle. He held it up to the crown of thorns, then to the nailed hands and feet, and finally to the pierced side. He turned to the congregation and said, "God's love. I have nothing more to add." He blew out the candle and left. He was right; there was nothing more that he or any theologian could add to the Cross. There were no comeback lines. God loves us more...no comebacks.

What I learned as I journeyed through my wilderness was that although I could never truly comprehend or understand God's love, I knew He loved me more... This truth, more than any other, is what kept me going. This truth, more than any other, is what you will need to cling to in your darkest hour. You need to hold onto this truth and believe in it with every part of your being, even though you may not fully understand or be able to explain it. God loves you...MORE!

Just as the priest in the illustration above used the dim light of the candle to show just a glimpse of God's love, we can never see the whole picture of God's love, but by looking at Christ on the Cross, we can see a glimpse of what the love of God looks like.

"For God so loved the world that he gave his one and only Son..." – John 3:16

"But God demonstrates his own love for us in this: While we were still sinners, Christ died for us." – Romans 5:8

God loves us and shows his love despite what we are. He chooses to love us regardless of us being filthy in sin. He does not wait for us to repent a little or to start acting more like him. His starting point is love, regardless.

In the Old Testament book of Hosea, God gives us a living parable to illustrate this love. God gives Hosea, his loyal and faithful prophet, Gomer, as his wife. However, the shock of this matrimonial union is that Gomer is not a beautiful young virgin from an honorable family but a prostitute. The holy prophet marries the city prostitute in a biblical soap opera. Despite her mistakes and her past, while Gomer was still a prostitute living in sin, Hosea loved her and chose to take her as his wife. No matter what you have done, no matter what sin is currently in your life...God loves you more...no comebacks, no ifs, and no buts. He loves you before you come to your senses; he loves you before you repent and before you say "I do" to Him. He loves you while you are a prostitute. Just like Hosea, God loves you while you are still a sinner.

However, this is not the end of the soap opera. After they are married and have had children, Gomer is unfaithful and returns to her former life. God's love however is relentless in its pursuit. God instructs Hosea to return for Gomer and to pay off her debts and bring her back as his wife. Wow.

Hosea's love, and by implication God's love, transcends logic and looks beyond the unfaithfulness to bring Gomer back home. She returns not as a slave but as his wife. Take a moment to reflect on that. This is just a glimpse of God's love, a small piece illuminated by that little candle, and yet it's already so much more than most can comprehend.

God did not only pursue us when we were lost and give his only Son while the world was in sin, but God still loved the world and pursued them after they rejected his Son. God remains faithful despite our unfaithfulness; even when we keep returning to our sinful past nature. God loves us...more!

I don't know where today's message sits with you.Perhaps, like Gomer, you are living a broken life. You are a prostitute to the things of this world. You think that nobody can love you and that you have drifted too far. God loves you more. He stands at the door of your heart knocking; he relentlessly pursues you despite your story, wanting you as his bride.

My guess, however, is that, like Gomer, you have experienced this love. You have accepted Christ and entered a relationship with Him, but something has gone wrong. You have been unfaithful. You are suffocated by your guilt and believe that there is no turning back now. You still love Christ, but your eyes have drifted back to the things of the world. You love the world and seek its pleasures. You have betrayed and broken this sacred covenant.

The truth is God still loves you...more. He will continue to pursue you even though you have been unfaithful. He still sees you as his bride; he still hopes that you will be ready when he comes back and that you will return home by his side. Can you get a small sense of how great His love for you is? It is this love that moves you to repentance; any other repentance is futile and passing. This love alone is all that can lead you to rebirth and revival; without it, you will continue to wander in the desert, merely surviving. Repentance and revival can only happen once you catch a glimpse of this love.

You are in the desert, not because God needs to punish you for your unfaithfulness. No, to the contrary, your path through the desert is for you to experience just a glimpse of God's compassion and to grasp this truth:

God loves you more...no comebacks!

Day 20: Cowbells and Gold Medals

If you could capture the perfect sights and sounds of Switzerland in a single image, it would have to be some cows heading out to pasture on the green slopes beneath snow-capped mountains and hearing the clanging sound of their cowbells in the distance. The Swiss will tell you that the reason they have such delicious chocolate and cheese is the fact that they have happy cows. I don't know how happy I would be to carry a heavy cowbell around my neck the whole day and hear that loud clonk every time I made the slightest move.

In recent years, the cowbell has become a popular souvenir at the Winter Olympics, and you will often find the crowds clanging these bells as they cheer the athletes on.

Now, picture winning a race at the Olympic Games, and instead of accepting the gold medal, you decided to hang a cowbell around your neck. I bet it won't remain hanging around your neck for very long. That click, clack, clonk continuously in your ear will most definitely leave you with a proper headache. I feel that this is exactly what we as Christians love doing; instead of wearing the gold medal that Christ has freely given us, we prefer to don a noisy cowbell. This cowbell is a constant reminder of our past sins and faults. The devil keeps using it to condemn us and remind us that we are not worthy of being children of God.

The final truth that we need to reaffirm as we wander through the wilderness is:

I know God has already forgiven me; the debt has been paid in full.

We exchange the gold medal that Christ has given us for the clanging cowbell of guilt and condemnation. We wear this constant reminder that we will never measure up. This is something that we cannot let pass and move forward from. The guilt and insecurity always remain, and when we do stumble, it clangs even louder as it confirms our greatest fears.

You may believe that Christ has died for your sins, but this cowbell around your neck constantly tells you something else. You may believe that you are called to be God's hands and feet in this world, but this cowbell tells you something different. However, Scripture teaches us that God wants us to forget what is behind us and leave it in the desert. He has made us new.

> *Forget the former things; do not dwell on the past. See, I am doing a new thing! Now it springs up; do you not perceive it? I am making a way in the wilderness and streams in the wasteland.* – Isaiah 43:18-19

> *Forgetting what is behind and straining toward what is ahead, I press on toward the goal to win the prize for which God has called me heavenward in Christ Jesus* – Philippians 3:13-14

What was in the past needs to be left there. Instead, we should press forward to receive the prize or the gold medal that Christ wants us to wear. This gold medal shows the world that there is victory over our sins and failures through Christ Jesus. So, what do you choose to wear around your neck? Do not let the devil lie to you; you are already forgiven, and you are already chosen.

In the book of Corinthians, Paul teaches us the difference between worldly repentance and true repentance (2 Corinthians

7:10). The consequence of worldly repentance is condemnation. We walk around carrying this cowbell, and even though we are sorry and feel condemned, we continue to stumble and fall under its weight. In contrast, the evidence of true repentance is not condemnation but rather conviction. We are convicted of our failings, and we turn from our ways through the new strength that now lives within us, the Holy Spirit. We then press on to receive the gold medal that Christ has destined us for.

One of my favorite Bible stories as a child was that of Zacchaeus, and if you are not immediately familiar with the name, you should remember this song... "Zacchaeus was a wee little man, and a wee little man was he...He climbed up into the Sycamore tree for the Lord he wanted to see." Being the shortest kid in the class, I could relate to old Zacchaeus.

Zacchaeus was a tax collector (something else we have in common). Now, tax collectors were real bad guys and rightly hated by the Jews. They not only worked for the cruel Roman government and were thus considered traitors, but they would steal from the people by charging amounts over and above the taxes due. They would get away with this as they were under the protection of the Romans. So, for the Jews, taxpayers were in their very own class as sinners. They were even worse than sinners.

It was more than just mere curiosity that led Zacchaeus to climb the tree to see Jesus. He was a wealthy man with everything he wanted, but he was still empty. He was hoping that by seeing Jesus and hearing Jesus, this void in him could be filled. Jesus can see his heart and recognizes that Zacchaeus is truly seeking Him. Jesus stops at the tree and invites himself to Zacchaeus' house. After this encounter, Zacchaeus gives half of his possessions to the poor and repays those whom he has stolen from four times over.

He is not just led to condemnation but rather conviction. He does not just put on this cowbell of condemnation but is convicted to change his ways, and his actions prove this conviction. He is free to forget the past and bury it. The void inside him has now been filled by Christ, and he is able to press on to receive the prize, the gold medal.

I don't know exactly where this all lands with you, but what is important is that while on our journey through the desert, we realize that to move forward, we will need to let go of the past. We cannot come out of the desert unless we are willing to and choose to drop this cowbell that continues to discount what Christ has done in us. Our past does not define us; it teaches us. What part of your past are you still clinging to? What part of your past is keeping you in the desert?

Never forget.

God has already forgiven you; the debt has been paid in full.

Part 3: Repentance

What's love got to do with it?

> *Haven't you experienced how kind and understanding He has been to you? Don't mistake His tolerance for acceptance. Do you realize that all the wealth of his extravagant kindness is meant to melt your heart and lead you to repentance?* – Romans 2:4b (TPT)

In this next section, we are invited to be moved to repentance. The repentance that I am talking about is much more than a mere admission of guilt and the resolve to do better. That is worldly repentance. The Godly repentance that we seek is where the desire to sin is buried with the sin and left in the desert. I know that is what we all want.

The problem with repentance is not so much its sincerity but rather its source. Growing up in church, we are given two choices: either one chooses to burn in hell for eternity, or you can decide to join a choir of angels in heaven. No prizes for guessing what every kid chooses. We are moved to repentance by the fear of what will happen if we don't repent. However, what happens to this repentance when the fear subsides? It, too, fades away, and we return to our old ways; the only way to keep people in repentance mode is by continually preaching fear.

The same principle applies to guilt; we do something bad and feel horrible. We are moved to repentance by this guilt and commit to never do it again. The problem is that as soon as the guilt subsides, so too does the repentance vanish, and we find ourselves doing the same thing. Eventually, the more we do this, the less guilty we feel and, consequently, the less we desire repentance.

So, what's love got to do with repentance? The truth is that repentance born out of fear or guilt is evanescing and short-lived. It is there in the morning but has evaporated by night. This is what some refer to as worldly repentance. The alternative is when we are moved to repentance by something that lasts forever...Love. Our repentance needs to be born from our encounter with and our experience of the love of Christ. As this love endures, so too will the repentance that comes from it. It lasts and does not wither away. That is why it is important to reaffirm and truly experience God's love in the wilderness before repentance. When we experience just a glimpse of Christ's love, we are moved to repentance and have no desire to go back to our old lives.

In the next few chapters, I want you to view repentance through the lens of God's love and His promises, which we reaffirmed in the second part of this book. Our repentance is an important step as we seek to exit the wilderness, but it must be Godly repentance that originates in love, not in fear or guilt.

My prayer is that over the next few chapters, you will be convicted to repent and leave your old self in the desert, not because I have been able to guilt you into that change or because I have managed to scare you with the consequences of non-compliance but rather that in your trials and your pain you have experienced the loving embrace of Christ and no longer what to go back to what you were... I pray that you experience enduring repentance that leads to revival the way God intended it.

"The Lord is close to all whose hearts are crushed by pain, and he is always ready to restore the repentant one." – Psalm 34:18 (TPT)

Day 21: **What's in the closet?**

It's been said that opposites attract, and my wife and I couldn't be more different when it comes to tidiness, which has sometimes resulted in heated debates over the years. I don't mind an empty coffee cup or sports cap lying about, but Brenda won't tolerate that, especially in the reception areas of our home. I often stoke the fire by telling her she needs a pair of homes: a show house for visitors and our main residence to live in. That does not amuse her.

Now, our confession...unbeknown to our guests admiring the impeccable tidiness of every room in sight, there is this one closet as you enter our humble abode that is not so pretty. This is where we stuff anything and everything that needs to be moved out of sight. From unused wrapping paper and ribbons to pillows and fall décor that got stored there as Christmas rolled by, to items that are waiting to be returned to the store but have made this closet their temporary home, to old computers and battery chargers that are hoarded there until we find a way to dispose of them.

Even though our home may appear picture perfect, we still have a bit of ugly in this closet. So, the question for you today is this...What's in your closet? Not the closet in your home but that of your heart. We often portray this perfect Instagram-able life, but in that closet, we hide the ugly that we do not want others to see.

That said, though we may tolerate and excuse a little chaos in our storage closet at home, God cannot and will not accept the dirt in our hearts. Do not mistake His tolerance for acceptance. We may convince ourselves that it is not so bad and that it does not harm anyone, but the spirit of God cannot live in the same space as our junk.

Light and darkness cannot co-inhabit our hearts.

Yes, God has a plan for us and wants to work through us, but he will not hesitate to burn the whole house down, even if there is just a little bit of junk in the closet. It doesn't matter if we live perfect Christian lives and say all the perfect Christian things; if we have any unforgiven sin that we just keep tolerating and refuse to eradicate, we will be exposed and destroyed. We are tools that God just cannot use because He cannot enter our hearts. Understand that what I'm referring to here is specifically the sin that we tolerate and bury in our hearts, the sin that we refuse to deal with.

While studying the book of Exodus, I came across three verses that deeply disturbed me and were extremely difficult for me to stomach because they were so convicting. I knew I had been called by God to reach people and lead them through their desert, much like Moses. All my life, He had prepared me for this moment, and I was finally ready to pursue his purpose for my life. Then I read these verses, and it felt like a piercing blade through my gut.

God was not going to use me; even worse, he could not use me. Because even though I was willing to tolerate and ignore the sin in my heart, he could not. It was non-negotiable. Either I dealt with the lust, pride, and resentment in me that I had learned to so masterfully masquerade and hide, or he would have no reservations in burning the whole house down. We need to be clear about this: God is serious about sin.

You may be familiar with the story of Moses, but allow me to briefly highlight how God handpicked him to lead the Israelites from the bondage of slavery to the Promised Land.

So, you have the enslaved nation of Israel. God hears their cries and makes a way for their deliverance through the birth and positioning of Moses, who was spared as a baby and found by Pharaoh's daughter while drifting down the Nile in a basket. This was God's perfect plan.

Although not named in Scripture, most scholars who trace the exodus from Egypt to the earlier date (1446BC) concur that this woman was likely Hatshepsut, the daughter of the Pharaoh at that time. Intriguingly, it is also understood that she could not bear children, and her husband, Pharaoh Thutmose, had a son by another woman who became the legal heir to the throne. So, in the context of this backdrop, could it have been God's initial plan to have Moses rise to the Egyptian throne or, at the very least, rise to a position of power as Joseph had done in the past?

To answer this would be mere speculation because as the story unfolds, Moses must flee from Egypt after murdering an Egyptian. Moses' sin eliminates any prospect of him rising to power in Egypt, and his choice to sin removes this plan or option from the table. What are the consequences of our choices and willful sin? Are we hampering God's plan for our own lives? The good news for us is that God does not give up on Moses, and neither will He give up on us.

Despite our sins, God continues to pursue us and fulfill His plans for our lives. What is important here is not whether Moses would have become king of Egypt but rather that God still chooses to use Moses, the murderer, to fulfill His plan to liberate His people. He does the same for you and me today, and we are moved to repentance because of how His love pursues us.

But that is not all... God not only chooses to still use Moses, but He also goes even further, choosing to equip and protect Moses by leading him into the wilderness to learn the ways of the wilderness. I am quite sure that his knowledge of the desert would have come in quite handy when he would later have two million people following him through this desert. God also protects Moses by providing him with family and security through his meeting with Jethro.

When Moses meets God in the form of a burning bush, God makes known His plan for Moses to liberate Israel. Moses tries in vain to get out of this, but this is what he was born to do even though he felt that he was not fit to do this and had disqualified himself. This is his purpose, and arguing with God was not going to change that. What struck me with this debate between God and Moses was that even though God uses our talents and strengths to serve Him, when He needs us to do something big...He will use our weaknesses. Eventually, Moses reluctantly agrees to go see the Pharaoh.

On his way to Egypt, hidden in Exodus 4:24-26 we find these three verses that caused me so much distress. God plans to kill Moses. What? Why would God go to all the trouble of preparing Moses for this anointed time and then just want to kill him? How does this even make sense? The reason is simple...God would not and still does not tolerate and accept disobedience. You guessed it, Moses has some dirt in the closet that he is unwilling to get rid of.

Moses and his wife, Zipporah, had failed to circumcise their son. The reasons and assumptions surrounding this are not important and speculative at best; what is important is that Moses remained disobedient to the covenant law and chose not to correct it. Maybe he thought this wasn't a big deal... But God, however, would not tolerate it.

Moses was not going to get a free pass just because he was called by God. God was not going to allow Moses to walk into his calling while he was still carrying this baggage. God would prefer to kill Moses than to tolerate his disobedience, even if Moses may have thought that this was not a deal breaker.

Many of us cannot walk into our calling because we refuse to let go of that thing holding us back, our baggage, our junk in the closet. Offense, Pride, Lust, Resentment, Unforgiveness,

Anger, or Fear. We tell ourselves that it's not a big deal. We can still praise and worship, we can still love, and we can still lead. It is just a minor issue that won't affect our ministry. But God won't tolerate this secret sin in us that we cling to. God does have a plan for us...but there is no room for this junk that we casually refuse to let go of.

Is it time to clean out the closet? Have you experienced his love and his relentless pursuit of you while you were still in sin?

What may seem as not that big of a deal to you could be the deal breaker.

Day 22: **Heart Matters**

"Repent! Repent! Repent or face the wrath of God!
Coming soon to a city near you...
The Minor Prophets."

Don't miss this opportunity to see them live and hear their riveting message of pending judgment and the call to repentance. Will you listen? Will you turn from your ways and seek God? Or will you choose to ignore them and cross over to the other side of the road?

The truth is Jonah, Amos, Joel, and their friends have been visiting our cities for thousands of years with this same message, but we have constantly chosen to continue in our own ways. Repentance may be the major message of these minor prophets, but if we stop and listen closely, we will soon discover that the repentance they preach is not just saying sorry and promising never to do it again. It is not about being "good" enough and abiding by all the religious fanfare that we have created. It is more than that. It is ultimately all about the heart.

As we experience God's love and draw close to him, we soon realize that God is frankly not interested in our external Christian rituals because He looks much deeper within. Neither our songs nor our offerings, our penance nor our pious

117

prayers move Him. His only concern is our hearts; that is all that matters. God does not accept or value our lip service and religious rituals as repentance and worship. We may be able to fool others with our "Christian ways," and sadly, we may even con ourselves, but not God. True repentance and, ultimately, true worship are a heart matter.

As I mentioned in the previous chapter, God takes sin seriously, and thus, one can expect the fire-and-brimstone preaching of these minor prophets, but it is not their intention to scare us into temporary repentance. Once we look past their fiery words we discover the heart of their message. God does not seek our sacrifice or offerings but rather our hearts and our love (Hosea 6:6).

Seeing as these minor prophets have traveled so far to come to our city today, let us stop and listen to what they have to say. The prophet Joel pleads with us to return to the Lord, but upon reflection, the petitions are not merely a plea to return to God with our external worship and words. Returning to the Lord means rendering or offering our hearts. This "rendering of the heart" is a deep inward expression and commitment, not just an outward ritual or custom that is offered by hypocrites.

> *'Even now,' declares the LORD, 'return to me with <u>all your heart</u>, with fasting and weeping and mourning.' <u>Rend your heart and not your garments</u>. Return to the LORD your God, for he is gracious and compassionate, slow to anger and abounding in love, and he relents from sending calamity.* – Joel 2:12-13

What Joel is referring to here is the outward expression of tearing one's garments in a time of distress and lament. We see this throughout the Old Testament when God's people are moved to remorse; they tear their clothes and cover their heads with ashes so that everyone can see they are mourning and in despair. It is of no benefit that we tear our garments to show the world that we are sorry but have no remorse in our hearts. I know that in our modern culture, tearing our trendy and expensive apparel may not be a thing, but you know what I am saying here. Outward expressions of repentance are in vain if not accompanied by the rendering of one's heart.

The message is clear: one should rather save your garment and tear open your heart.

Next up, the prophet Amos goes a step further as he deals with one's "rendered heart." One can expect the rendered heart of the truly repentant sinner to bear certain fruit, specifically love for one's neighbor. During the time of Amos, Israel was experiencing a major "boom" in its economy. It was probably the most prosperous time during the divided kingdom of Israel. People lived in abundance, or as we would say today, they were "so blessed." Were they religious? Yes, they continued to take their offerings to the temple and celebrate religious feasts, but things were different in their hearts.

Amos calls them out for the social injustices and the way they treat the poor and underprivileged. Their actions do not reflect the heart of a truly repentant sinner. This angers God. Their empty faith and worthless religious ceremony, but mostly their total disregard for the needs of the poor and downtrodden. Does that sound like our world today? If so, here is a message from God:

> *I hate, I despise your religious festivals; your assemblies are a stench to me. Even though you bring me burnt offerings and grain offerings, I will not accept them. Though you bring choice fellowship offerings, I will have no regard for them. Away with the noise of your songs! I will not listen to the music of your harps. But let justice roll on like a river, righteousness like a never-failing stream! Did you bring me sacrifices and offerings forty years in the wilderness, people of Israel?* – Amos 5:21-25

Amos makes it very clear how God feels about empty worship and our worldly repentance. Like the people of Israel, we too have religion; we practice our "faith," so why would God reject this? Because our hearts are not moved by the social injustices around us, and we turn a blind eye to the suffering of others. This reminds me of the story of the Jews in Germany being transported by train to their death in the concentration camps. As the train passes a small church, they start screaming and pleading for mercy and help. What do you think the congregation did? They just started worshipping and singing louder to drown out these pleas. What are we trying to drown out today? Be still, my friend; God speaks to us in the silence of our hearts. A repentant heart is always moved by the brokenness in the world, for it, too, once was broken.

Lastly, I would like us to stop and listen to Jonah. We all know Jonah, he is the guy that got swallowed by the fish. He is kind of like the main act of the minor prophet roadshow. His stories are sure to pull in the crowds. However, Jonah does not want to tell us about his time in the belly of the fish, or about *"those"* people of Nineveh. He wants us to know that even Godly men and prophets struggle with matters of the heart.

Even after the whole fish episode, Jonah concedes and goes to Nineveh but is still very reluctant and unenthusiastic. The best he can do is a one-line sermon that he goes around mumbling through the streets of Nineveh. Jonah has a heart problem. He wants to see the sinful people of Nineveh rightly punished, and he wants them to get what they deserve. He does not want them to be forgiven. He hopes his half-hearted preaching will not sway the people to repent, thus leading to God's wrath over them, but he discovers that God will even use our half-hearted attempts to make miracles.

Jonah writes his book so that we can see him not as some holy guy who followed God but rather as someone who had a heart problem and was unwilling to forgive. Jonah is honest enough to admit this grave failing in him as he sits under that withering tree, sulking. God's desire is not that we fill our hearts with resentment and unforgiveness, no matter how justified that anger and resentment are. When we offer or render our hearts completely to God, there is no room for resentment.

The heart of the repentant sinner will always be slow to anger and quick to forgive. So, let us tear open our hearts in the next few chapters and discover what needs to be flushed out.

Day 23: The Magic Coin

The world sure has changed in the last forty years. When I was a kid growing up in South Africa, the only video games we knew were the old arcade machines at the local corner shop. From the classic Pac-man to Street Fighter II, twenty cents got you enough credits to keep you busy for some time.

When these coin arcade machines first became popular, one of my dad's close friends was the first to invest in them in our small town, and he literally struck gold. His convenience store was located right across from the public swimming pool and within walking distance of several schools. Students would line up after school to play, and soon, he must have had at least fifteen arcade machines.

He was cashing in for some time, but soon revenue from the machines began to drop at an alarming rate. At first, he thought the children were getting too good at the games and taking longer to finish their allotted credits. The place remained busy with children playing the games all afternoon, but revenue continued to plummet. He could not understand what was going on until one kid confessed that everyone was using a "magic coin," which unlocked unlimited credits.

Those first arcade machines were not very sophisticated, and one of the kids soon figured out that a standard nut washer was roughly the same size as the twenty-cent coin, and if one tied the nut washer to some string, you could pull it back up out of the machine. Once you had run out of credits, you would simply drop the washer into the machine again, unlock more credits, and pull the "magic coin" up again. This was great news for students with limited finances, as they had now unlocked a way to gain "uncapped, unlimited screen time for free, forever." Predictably, by the following week, all the arcade games had been removed from the store.

The reason I bring up this story is that I truly believe that many of us think of our repentance prayer as our very own magic coin that gives us access to repetitive, uncapped grace. We are now free to sin as much as we like because we have this magic coin attached to a string that we just keep inserting into the arcade machine to unlock more credits. In the end, we still get to go to heaven, so how we live our lives now is irrelevant.

Paul addresses this very issue in his letter to the Romans, chapter 6, where he poses the rhetorical question, "Are we to continue in sin that grace may abound?" or placed within the context of the story above, "Are we going to continue dropping the magic coin into the arcade machine, as the store owner is just happy to have us there?" Paul's answer is an immediate and emphatic "Absolutely not!"

Paul challenges us to reflect on what he taught concerning grace and, in so doing, flush out any misconceptions or misunderstandings. Paul knows that many who hear his teaching of God's abounding grace will be tempted to bend it to justify their selfish motives. He knows that his teaching about how grace will always surpass sin will give some of his hearers a "license to sin." Paul irrevocably rejects this thought. By raising the question and immediately rejecting even the thought thereof, Paul shows how crazy and ludicrous this idea is...Yet, for some of us, the idea of uncapped, unlimited grace time remains very enticing.

So, what am I saying? Is God's grace capped? Does He forgive up to a certain point and then remove the arcade games in anger? Absolutely not! What God does when you truly repent and are baptized is give you a new heart. A heart that is no longer motivated by the temporary thrills of arcade games nor by using a dirty magic coin to get the best deal. A heart that seeks to serve, to give, and to love. A heart that seeks God's kingdom first. This new heart that is born from true repentance and baptism with Christ cannot continue or remain in sin.

The baptism that Paul preaches in Romans 6 is not merely being dunked in a baptismal pool in front of a cheering and supportive congregation; no, his readers in Rome understand baptism as publicly attaching or binding oneself to this crucified King and thus pledging allegiance to Him. It meant publicly rejecting the faith of your family and rejecting earthly rulers like Ceasar. As a result, this baptism would inevitably mark one for persecution. A death wish, if you will.

Biblical scholars associate the meaning of the word *"baptizo"* with the process of permanently dyeing one's clothes. There is no going back to the old garment once the robe has been immersed in the dye. The old color is gone, and only the new one is now visible. True repentance and baptism mean a "newness" to our lives. What Paul is trying to illustrate is that if you have died to sin, through your baptism, you can no longer live in sin. We are liberated from the penalty of sin through Christ's blood on the Cross, but furthermore, we are also set free from the power of sin by the death of our old selves with Him through baptism (Watchman Nee). Sin is no longer our master. Paul is not teaching us that we will never sin again but rather that we are no longer under the rule, authority, or power of our old master, Sin.

As Sméagol was corrupted by his precious magic ring in The Lord of the Rings, have we, too, been corrupted by our precious magic coin? Are we okay with our sin because we have uncapped credits? This is what the theologian Dietrich Bonhoeffer refers to as "cheap grace" in his book, The Cost of Discipleship. As he puts it, this cheap grace is the enemy of our church. It deals with the sin but does nothing for the sinner who continues in sin.

The sinner has a magic coin with unlimited credits; he no longer needs to turn from his sinful ways and become a disciple by following the way. This cheap grace is killing the church as it only addresses the sin and does not deal with the sinner; it takes care of the symptoms but not the cause.

In contrast, Bonhoeffer describes "Costly grace" as being costly because it costs a man his whole life, but also grace as it gives that man the only true life. Read that again and think about it. The grace you are seeking will cost you everything, your whole life, but in return, give you everything...true life. The grace we are seeking is not in the magic coins we are hiding in our pockets; that is only a sweet deal for us, but it robs the store owner.

Don't be fooled and misled; don't settle for cheap grace. Instead, seek this costly grace by accepting the full price that was paid, but also be prepared to pay the cost of your old self dying on that Cross with Christ. If we choose cheap grace, we shouldn't be alarmed when the arcade games are removed, and we are left behind with nothing but a nut washer on a string. Nothing magical about that ending.

Day 24: **No way I'm wearing that!**

Some of us are just sports enthusiasts and fanatical about the teams we support. Nothing evokes passion and raw emotion like team sports, and watching adult men lose their minds over their team's poor performance on the field can be quite entertaining. I can also get a little "loco" about my beloved Liverpool Football Club, so there is no judgment here. Nothing makes or breaks my weekend more than the outcome of the Liverpool match. Although it can lift my mood, it also inevitably brings out the worst in me.

You may be familiar with the phrase "Good ol' fashioned hate." Well, this was my introduction to college football when I first moved to the States. An important note to self: You should never mistake a Georgia Tech fan for a Bulldog. They are not the same team, and let's just say that they have a bit of a frosty rivalry going on, much like my feelings about Manchester United and Manchester City. I just don't like them. I admit that. Too many painful losses to them over the years. I support Liverpool and any team playing against Manchester.

If I have learned anything in the desert, it is that God sometimes has a strange way of getting His point across, so you can imagine my complete horror when He put an image in my mind of me wearing a Man United top. Even worse, I was wearing it with so much pride and justifying it. I still get cold shivers just thinking about it. I was distraught, but what was the point God was trying to convey with this unsettling image?

I believe that He wanted me to understand what it looks like when I choose to don the devil's team jersey. What do I mean? When we act contrary to what God commands, we put on a jersey that does not represent Him. We wear the rival team's colors, and we wear it with pride. We sometimes even feel the need to justify why it is okay for us to wear the rival's jersey. When we choose to knowingly act in a way that is contrary to that which God has called us to do, then we choose to don Satan's team colors. This is especially true when it comes to how we deal with offense and bitterness.

When somebody offends us or hurts our feelings, we somehow believe it is okay to walk around being offended or bitter, but is this what love requires of you? We are rightfully upset and fully justified with our anger, but by choosing not to let go of this offense and by clinging onto it, we are putting on our rival's team jersey and waving their flag. We know that these feelings are from the devil, but we keep wearing his team jersey and defending our stance. We simply refuse to just let it go.

Make no mistake, our offense is from the devil, and he uses it skillfully to try and destroy the relationships in the body of Christ. The reason that offense is such an effective tool is that it is a double-edged sword; it not only harms the parties that are involved by taking root in their hearts and growing into bitterness, but it also hurts those who look up to you. Our choice to entertain the offense and justify our feelings while we profess to be followers of Christ is confusing. It pushes people away from Jesus. It discredits our testimony. I may say I support Liverpool and may even passionately preach it, but if you see me in a Manchester shirt, you won't believe me. We can preach Jesus all day, but if we choose to wear a cloak of offense and bitterness, that is what all people will see, and they cannot take our pious words seriously.

We need to rid ourselves of offense because by clinging onto it, we are not only hurting ourselves, but we are harming the entire body of Christ. Offense happens; this is inevitable. We will be offended, and we will offend, too; however, what is most important is how we choose to deal with this offense. Do we choose to wear this jersey or not? Now, I appreciate that your situation is different and that if I had given you a chance to explain yourself, your feelings would have been justifiable. But it does not change the need to rid yourself of this offense. Not doing so will result in it completely consuming you and turning you bitter.

One of my first ventures into business was a partnership in a restaurant with a very close friend. He was Greek, and I was Portuguese. The partnership was largely successful because even though we had disagreements, we worked through them without taking offense until one day when I had had enough. I was offended, justifiably or not, and I refused to just let it go. My offense caused him to be offended in return, and it was a downhill spiral from there. A good partnership and friendship went down the drain.

Still, I refused to let it go and carried this offense with me. Gradually, it began to transform into bitterness and resentment. About a year later, I was watching the Greek national soccer team play, and I remember cheering for the opposition and wanting Greece to lose. My reason...I knew this would annoy and frustrate him. I had nothing against Greece but secretly just wanted him to be miserable. I was shocked at how low I had fallen; Satan had a hold of my heart, and it was overgrown with bitterness. I knew then I had to find a way to let Christ intervene and help me let go of this resentment. These same feelings of offense and being overcome with bitterness and resentment are exactly what led the religious leaders to eventually crucify Christ. These same feelings may be in you as well.

Offense never ends well, and it has a way of really tripping us up. For me, repentance meant removing Satan's team jersey and tearing open my heart to be cleansed by the Holy Spirit of all the offense, bitterness, and resentment that I had stockpiled there for so long despite being a follower of Christ.

Do not repay anyone evil for evil. Be careful to do what is right in the eyes of everyone. If it is possible, as far as it depends on you, live at peace with everyone. - Romans 12: 17-18

There is so much packed into these verses, but I just want to touch on a few points. "Do not repay anyone evil for evil." It has become a cultural norm to demand payback and get even. We are encouraged to take offense and settle the score. However, The Passion Translation (TPT) puts this part of verse 17 very simply and bluntly: "Never hold a grudge or try to get even." If you have truly experienced Godly repentance, then it becomes nearly impossible to hold a grudge or demand to get even because you understand the liberating power of forgiveness. Stop and read that again.

God knows that sometimes it may not be possible to live at peace with everyone, but He does not want you to be the reason that it is not possible. Sometimes, this peace is not possible for us because the wound has cut too deep, but if we can surrender this to Christ, he can and will bury it in the desert. This may take time, but we will be able to find peace through Christ.

The original Greek for peace used in this text is *"eirēneuontes,"* which means the permanent act of laying down all one's weapons, it is not just a temporary ceasefire where we are still clinging to our guns and ready to resume the battle. We permanently destroy our artillery, and we refuse to be at war any longer.

We need to drop Satan's team jersey and put on Christ's jersey of peace and love so that all who witness and see us will know for sure whose team we are on. God needs you to stop holding on to these things that are holding you back. For you to get through this desert, you need to let go of all offense.

Day 25: Hidden Agenda

We may often feel as though we spend more time in meetings than we do working our actual jobs. We have planning meetings in preparation for a meeting and then arrange debrief meetings to discuss what was discussed at the meeting. Attending meetings may seem like all we do for a living, and we soon learn that a meeting without a clear agenda is typically a waste of time. However, we should be more concerned by the agenda that is not on the actual agenda. The hidden agenda.

In my desert wanderings over the past few years, the frequency of my meetings with my Creator has increased, and it was during one of these late-night meetings that my hidden agenda was brought to light with a simple question... "Joel, why have you chosen to follow me?"

I knew what the answer should be, and I knew what I wanted the answer to be, but in truth the answer was... Me. I was following Jesus because ultimately there was something in it for me. That was hard to admit and as we sit at a crossroads in our wilderness journey, you are faced with this question as well... My friend, why have you chosen to follow Jesus?

What is your true motive for following? Is it all just about *you* getting to heaven, or are you hopeful that signing on as a disciple will guarantee you a better life? Go on then, what is really on your agenda?

Our hidden agenda is often the very thing that we need to reveal when it comes to repentance. It is not just about confessing our evil ways and sinful choices; repentance starts by bringing ourselves, our selfish desires, and our hidden agenda to the Cross. Our self-seeking motives and our veiled ambitions need to be nailed to the Cross. We need to confess and repent of our instinctive and natural predisposition to serve "self." If not, we may find ourselves stuck in the desert for a while longer.

This may be hard teaching, but we desperately need teaching that makes us uncomfortable. We find it much easier to preach about things that are uplifting and encouraging, it is never really a convenient time to preach about the real problem, self and its hidden agenda. We need to repent of "self" and leave our personal agenda in the wilderness, and the timing is never convenient.

I want to introduce you to a man named Felix, who was the governor of Judea around the time when Paul was arrested in Acts 23. You might relate to Felix; he had worked hard to get to the top and was now enjoying the fruit of his labor. He had power, wealth, influence, and status. We discover that Felix was not opposed to hearing "the good news" and was no stranger to this "new way," but his job as a governor was his priority and focus. Felix had some skeletons in his closet, too, like most politicians, and unsurprisingly, he, too, had a hidden agenda. He was also very cunning in leveraging his powers to promote his personal agenda in every situation.

Now, the apostle Paul's case comes before Felix in Caesarea, and he hears the accusations brought against Paul and the defense. To buy some time, Felix deliberately delays judgment until the arresting officer can make it to Caesarea to testify. Sounds noble, but we, as readers, suspect he may have an ulterior agenda.

The Scripture tells us that Felix was "well acquainted with the way," so he already had an encounter with and an understanding of this new Christian faith. He was well aware of the good that these Christians were doing and that their faith was not against any law. Felix was also specifically intrigued by Paul. He had questions and a desire to learn more, but he first wanted to assess what could be in it for him. He arranges to have Paul meet with him and his wife, Drusilla, who is a Jew, to discuss this new way and answer their questions.

Felix decides to entertain Paul's teachings about Christ with the hopes of identifying if this "new way" could advance his political agenda or, at the very least, give rise to the opportunity to solicit a bribe. Felix's motives are centered around self. He doesn't mind the gospel, he does not oppose it, and he is keen on the benefits that the gospel brings to his jurisdiction, but he is more concerned about what is in it for him.

Many of us are like Felix, too; we are genuinely only concerned with our interests. What can we get out of following Christ? If we are going to surrender our lives, what can we expect in return for ourselves? Eternity in Heaven? Current earthly blessings? Let's reflect on a different question to make the point. If following Christ offered no earthly blessings nor the promise of eternity in heaven, would you still follow Him despite the cost?

Remember me telling you about our friend Felix having some skeletons in the closet? Well, his wife Drusilla was already married when he met her, but they chose to pursue their lusts, and Felix enticed her away from her husband to marry him. Felix and Drusilla enjoyed listening to Paul's teaching, and his message captivated them. However, this quickly changes as Paul starts to convict them about their past, and the meeting gets a little uncomfortable. Felix has had enough and responds,

"That's enough for now! You may leave. When I find it convenient, I will send for you." – Acts 24:25

When convenient? Excuse me? Felix hears the truth but is not willing to change. It does not align with his agenda. It is not convenient for him to acknowledge his wrongdoing and repent. It is not convenient for him to accept the blood that was shed. It is not convenient for him to surrender his entire life, his possessions, his status, his ambitions, and his future to Christ. Well, how about us? Is now a convenient time?

God has a plan and a purpose for us, and He needs us to fully surrender to Him so that we can be His hands and feet in this world. We cannot continue to procrastinate on this decision until a more convenient time.

From a very young age, I felt God was calling me into his ministry, but I was afraid. For me, the ministry meant becoming a catholic priest, and that was neither appealing nor convenient. My dreams were more about finding love, getting married, and having children. So... I ran. God, however, did not discard me, and He granted me all my heart's desires and more. Still, He kept calling, but I kept running. It was never a convenient time.

Then came the wilderness, which would bring me to my knees but more importantly to His feet. As the world around me collapsed and I faced an uncertain future, but God still never stopped pursuing me.

"I know you don't want to hear this, but I've been praying, and I feel God is saying he wants you, Joel." These words were like a sword to my prideful heart. Brenda was right; God was still calling me, but I didn't want to hear that. It was not a convenient time and not on my agenda.

Months later, after many midnight meetings with God, I was finally ready to tear up my agenda and repent. Not my will but Yours. I was ready to surrender and answer His call. Everything I had been chasing, my whole agenda, was worthless, and I finally was able to grasp what Paul meant in his passionate letter to the Philippians:

> *Yet all of the accomplishments that I once took credit for, I've now forsaken them, and I regard it all as*

nothing compared to the delight of experiencing Jesus Christ as my Lord! To truly know him meant letting go of everything from my past and throwing all my boasting on the garbage heap. It's all like a pile of manure to me now. – Philippians 3:7-8 (TPT)

I didn't know where this road would lead and where God's plan would take our family, but I knew that there would never be a more convenient time than right then.

God is calling you today to surrender your life to Him completely. He may not be calling you to be a pastor, but we are all called to minister. We are all called to be His hands and feet in this world. Even if you have been a Christian for a while, maybe you are in the wilderness because God wants you, and you refuse to hear His call...Is now a convenient time?

Day 26: This Little Light of Mine

This little light of mine, I'm gonna let it shine... let it shine, let it shine, let it shine. I wonder what memories these lyrics bring up in your mind. Maybe they take you right back to your childhood, and you recall belting out this song repeatedly, Sunday after Sunday after Sunday. Whatever your memory, the message is as important today as it was back then. Christ is the light of the world, and we need to unashamedly take this light to every dark corner of the world.

Personally, these lyrics remind me of my youngest daughter's preschool concert. Her teacher decided it would be cute to give each child a small flashlight to shine around while singing the song, which was in the evening's repertoire. This sounds like a nice idea, but as always, the problem lies in the execution of the plan. As the lights dimmed for the kids to turn on the flashlights, half of them started screaming, afraid of the dark, and the rest became so enchanted with shining their little flashlights that they forgot to sing.

Jesus loves this visual imagery of light and darkness and uses it several times in his teachings. He knows that even the smallest little light has the power to drive out the darkness. In John 8:12, Jesus says, "I am the light of the world. Whoever follows me will never walk in darkness but will have the light of life." God intended that we carry this light and share it with the world; however, we have twisted this by using the light as a tool to condemn those in darkness.

"For God did not send His Son into the world to condemn the world, but to save the world through Him." – John 3:17

This is where many of us miss the heart of the Gospel and why we need repentance. Rather than applying the gospel as God intended—to show mercy and save the lost—we use it to judge and condemn the world.

We use the light of Christ like a flashlight, illuminating the shortcomings and faults of those around us. A flashlight is designed to force all the light in one direction, and therefore, none of the light from this flashlight shines back on us. We, as the bearers of the flashlight, remain in the dark.

This beautiful light of Christ becomes a weapon that use to attack and judge those in the darkness. We believe that as bearers of this light, we are okay, we are holy, and we have God's favor, but sadly, we are, in fact, left in the darkness as none of the light is shining on us. We are no better than the Pharisees who used the Law of Moses as a flashlight to high-light everyone's faults, but they were the ones truly in the dark, not being able to connect with God's intention for the law and being stuck on the legalities of the law.

Are we guilty of using the light of Christ, the Gospel, as a flashlight? Are we just modern-day "Christian Pharisees"? Are we in the darkness even though we carry the light?

"If we claim to have fellowship with him and yet walk in the darkness, we lie and do not live out the truth." – 1 John 1:6

Maybe this is why we are stuck in this wilderness. Maybe this is the area that requires repentance. We can all agree that God wants us to take His light into the world, but how we are doing this could be the problem.

Instead of carrying the light of Christ as a flashlight, we should rather carry it in a lamp or lantern. If we choose to carry Christ's light in a lantern, the light fills the entire room and chases out the darkness. We, who are carrying this lantern, are also covered by the light. All our failings, our faults, and our weaknesses are in the light and are exposed. Those who are in the dark see us, the imperfect light-bearers, in the light and no longer feel condemned. They are no longer ashamed and feel at ease to step into the light with us. They no longer need to run from the light. This is the way God intended for you to shine your little light... in a lantern and not as a flashlight.

All who do evil hate the light and refuse to go near it for fear their sins will be exposed. But those who do what is right come to the light, so others can see God at work in what they are doing. - John 3:20-21 (NLT)

Jesus wants us to stand in the light we are carrying and not just point the light around as a weapon. He called us out of darkness to experience His marvelous light, so we no longer stand behind the flashlight but rather hold up the lamp and stand in the light.

We read earlier from John 8:12, where Jesus says that He is the light of the world, and if we follow Him, we will no longer walk in darkness but have His light. To put this statement in context, we find a fascinating showdown between the Pharisees (the light-bearers) and Jesus (the true light of the world) in the preceding verses, John 8:1-11.

The religious leaders of the time were growing ever more frustrated with Jesus. His message of a loving and forgiving God did not align with their tried and tested way of instilling fear of the wrath of God. The Pharisees were desperate to trick Jesus into saying the law was wrong, which would discredit Him as a teacher, or alternatively, to have Him agree with the law, thereby contradicting his own message. They devise a plan and bring a woman, "caught" in the act of adultery, to Jesus, who is teaching at the temple, and ask him if it is right for them to stone her as prescribed by the Law of Moses.

It is important to note how they are using the law as a flash-light to accuse the woman but simultaneously breaking the law by dragging this allegedly unclean woman into the holy temple and then proposing to murder her in the temple, too. Also, what happened to the guy that was with the woman? Surely, it takes two to tango, right? In fact, according to the Law of Moses, which they are referencing, both the man and the woman caught in adultery should face the penalty of death. Conveniently, however, they only bring the woman be-fore Jesus as she has no right to a defense. These religious leaders have meticulously studied every minor detail of the law, so this is no oversight; they are purposely bending the law to suit their agenda. They are manipulating the flashlight to shine the light of the law only where they are directing it.

Jesus is aware of their manipulation and half-truths but chooses not to confront them, instead, he starts writing in the dirt and just says "Let him who is without sin, cast the first stone." What He was writing we are not told but maybe it was the exact wording of the law, or maybe he was writ-ing each of their transgressions. One by one they drop their stones and leave. The woman is left on her own and Jesus tells her to go and to sin no more.

Jesus does not condone her sin nor try to sweep it under the carpet. Adultery is a sin. Jesus knows this, everyone pres-ent knows this, and even the woman herself knows this. Jesus does not come to the woman's defense by trying to shift or spread the blame to her absent male accomplice. Jesus looks into her eyes, confronts her with love, and tells her to stop with her sinful ways. She does not feel condemned by being singled out and put under the spotlight. Instead, she is stand-ing in the light with Jesus. She is experiencing love, not judg-ment. In doing this, Jesus gives us a clear example of how to carry His light into the world in a lantern and not a flashlight.

Where do you tend to use the light of Christ as a flashlight? Who are those whose failings you keep pointing out with your flashlight? Is it perhaps those who are of a different faith?

When sharing the gospel with them, are you using a flashlight or a lantern? Maybe you struggle with another's race, culture, or political sentiments. It is easy to go around shining our flashlight at what everyone else is doing wrong, but in the process, our failings remain in the dark.

What about homosexuality? We are living in an era where society is encouraging the blurring of gender lines. How do we deal with that as followers of Christ? Do we shine a flashlight on it and start throwing stones? Or do we just filter out Scripture so as not to offend anyone and pretend there is nothing wrong? We should follow Christ's example by carrying His light in a lantern. His light is the truth that overcomes the darkness, not only in those with whom we share the light but, more importantly, within us.

Yes, homosexuality is against Scripture and God's will, but so is that secret lust that burns in my heart, so is that vanity with our own exterior image and the thoughts that make us look down on others, and so is that bitterness that hides behind our smiles and the envy that fuels my ambition. Let us not hide in the darkness but rather step into the light.

We should not ignore sin by only preaching the non-offensive, sugar-coated gospel, but neither should we use the light as a weapon and refuse to stand in that same light. Let's make a choice today to leave our flashlights behind in the desert and instead pick up our lanterns and let our little light shine...the way God desires for it to shine.

Day 27: **Saved from the Trash**

As parents of two beautiful girls, we have also inherited about a dozen or so baby dolls. No, these are not just toys that just sit on the shelf; these dolls have been an integral part of our family for the last few years. They each have their own name and personality, and they get changed several times a day into their latest fashionable gear. They have seats at the dinner table and join us on family outings as well. The problem comes once our two little princesses are asleep: Mom and Dad have to spend the rest of the evening packing away their babies and the mess they have made.

After a couple of unsuccessful attempts to teach our little girls the lost art of packing away toys and tidying up their mess, I knew I needed to be a little firmer. I resorted to grabbing a large trash bag and threatened that all unpacked toys would end up in the trash. This worked great for a while, but eventually, they saw through my idle threats. Soon, waving the trash bag around had no effect; they just ignored me.

Until that one day when this tranquil and carefree vibe quickly turned to panic as Dad started moving the toys from the floor into the trash bag, I will never forget my little Giana's face as she tried desperately to save her babies from ending up in the trash. Her attempts to gather and carry them to safety were in vain, as her little arms could not hold them all.

Mom offered to come to her aid, but the poor child was in such a frenzy panic that she refused the help, probably believing she could no longer trust either of her parents. As she was picking up her dolls, she kept dropping the ones in her arms, which, of course, elevated her anxiety and panic. She then tried grabbing more simultaneously as her mean father was getting closer, but the harder she tried, the less successful she was. Eventually, all the dolls were on the floor, and she sank down with them in a puddle of tears. Mom offered her help again, and having no other choice, our little girl reluctantly surrendered and accepted her mother's help.

I know none of you will now be nominating me for the "Dad of the Year" award, but to put you all at ease, all the babies were saved from the trash.

My daughter's reaction is not that bizarre, as many of us react similarly when dealing with our fears, anxiety, and stress. Her instinct when facing fear was to try and take control of the situation. She quickly worked herself up into such a panic that she was unable to accept help or surrender control. This same instinct is in all of us; we are unable to relinquish control. However, we soon learn as my daughter did, that when you refuse to surrender control, you eventually and inevitably end up losing control. You end up on the floor in a puddle of tears.

The "why" behind the desire to control and the refusal to surrender is precisely the reason we need repentance. Our default is to take matters into our own hands because of our inability to fully trust and rely on God in our moments of crisis. This is the problem.

By trying to micro-manage and control every possible outcome because you fear what might happen if you don't, you inevitably end up on the floor in a puddle of tears as it becomes too much to handle. Control is a vicious cycle that consumes you; the more you try to control every outcome, the more anxiety, worry, and fear you generate. The more anxiety, worry, and fear you have, the more you try and control every outcome. You never win.

Maybe this is what we need to leave behind in the desert. God wants us to let go of control and hand the steering wheel of our life over to Him before we completely lose control. By refusing to surrender our worries and fears to God, we are not putting our faith and trust fully in Christ. In the book of Proverbs, we are told to trust God with all our hearts and in every area of our lives; I particularly loved how this is translated in The Message:

> *Trust God from the bottom of your heart and don't try to figure out everything on your own. Listen for God's voice in everything you do, everywhere you go; He's the one who will keep you on track. Don't assume you know it all. Run to God! Run from evil!* - Proverbs 3:5-6 (MSG)

This verse applies to all of us, and even if you believe you don't have a problem relinquishing control, in a moment of crisis, your instinct will be to try and wrestle control back from God. For some of us, this desire to control is evident in our finances, while for others, it may be our children. We trust God, but there is a big bad world out there, and we need to take charge. The thing about surrendering to God is that it is all or nothing. You cannot surrender most areas of your life but cling to control over that one area that keeps you up at night. You either fully trust God or you don't.

If the desire to control is born out of fear, then the need to surrender is born out of trust. Your choice is not merely to control or surrender but rather a choice to fear an unknown future or trust a known God.

In Luke 4:1-13, Jesus is led by the Holy Spirit into the desert. The question is, why was Jesus led into the desert? To be tempted, yes, but why? I believe that it has to do with the choice to trust God or take control. Jesus is vulnerable and weak after spending forty testing days in the desert. The burden and sheer magnitude of his calling would have filled him with anxiety. This was Satan's goal, to have Jesus wrestle control back from God amid his crisis. But Jesus is wise to Satan's scheme and knows that fully trusting the Father means he must completely surrender to God's will and timing.

The first temptation deals with Jesus taking control of the situation to meet His physical needs. He had not eaten for forty days and was starving. He could take control of this crisis, by turning the stones into bread, but he realized that this would mean He was not trusting God to meet His needs. Are we perhaps tempted to take control of providing for ourselves, or do we trust God's faithfulness in providing for our families?

After this, Jesus is tempted to take control of the future by immediately ruling over the world. The devil is offering Jesus a shortcut to fulfilling his purpose to be king over all the world. God's plan involves Jesus becoming king via the Cross, but the devil offers a fast-forward way to the throne. Have you ever been tempted to take control of your circumstances by cutting corners or taking the easy alternative to God's plan?

Satan is relentless and tries for a third time to tempt Jesus to take control. He tries to sow doubt by arguing that people cannot believe Jesus is the Son of God. He quotes Scripture to substantiate why Jesus should take control of this doubt and prove to everyone that He truly is the Son of God. Satan affords Jesus the opportunity to prove to all the doubters that he is who he says he is by having God's angels come to his rescue. Jesus refuses to take control away from God but rather places all of His trust in God and the path that God has planned to show that He is the promised one. People may doubt you and your calling to follow Christ, and Satan will consistently remind you that you are not worthy. You may be tempted to take matters into your own hands but rather continue to trust Christ to be your intercessor and advocate.

When we are in the wilderness, the fire in our hearts starts to wane, and the promises that God has given us start to dim and fade. Questions and doubts begin to overtake our thoughts. Why has God led us into the desert to die? Why has he abandoned us? Did we really hear God's message correctly? Satan then comes and offers us an easy way out, a shortcut...All we need to do is take control of the situation, but in doing so, we fail the test of fully trusting in God.

So, what are the baby dolls that you are grasping onto and refusing to surrender? Will we choose to surrender control, or will we risk losing control by clinging on in desperation? Today, decide to trust God with your children, your finances, your health...or with that impossible situation. Today, decide to leave your need to control in the desert, to die, and to surrender complete control to God, or decide to continue wandering through the wilderness, clinging to control until you lose it and end up on the floor in a puddle of tears.

Day 28: **Honey-Do List**

I don't think this book would be complete if it didn't address the greatest journey through the desert, as recorded in the Old Testament book of Numbers. This book is known in the Jewish Torah as "Bamidbar," which translates literally as "In the Wilderness." Moses leads the liberated nation of Israel through the wilderness on a forty-year trek. As you find yourself in a spiritual desert, it could be beneficial to read this portion of the Old Testament and consider the lessons that can be drawn from the Israelites' journey.

The Israelites were not lost; God led them into the wilderness for a purpose, and this applies to your journey as well. God was not punishing the nation of Israel; He wanted to lead them to true repentance so that they would be able to discard their old, corrupt nature in the desert and demonstrate what was truly in their hearts.

The book of Numbers is so captivating, it starts like an action movie. Injustice, an unlikely hero, conflict, plagues, liberation, and the crossing of the Red Sea. Action, action, and more edge-of-seat action. But this high tempo comes to a screeching halt when they enter the desert. It is during this break in play that they start contemplating their circumstances. This "downtime" that was meant to help organize their camp for the battles ahead is the time when discontentment begins to rear its ugly head.

Up until chapter 10 of Numbers, everything progressed according to plan, but things began to unravel with the first line in chapter 11. The Israelites start doing something that truly angers God. They start complaining. In their defense, the Israelites seem to have some legitimate reasons for their gripe: they are stuck in a desert, it is hot as hell, and they must eat the same bland meal every single day. I would certainly not be a happy camper. Was God's overreacting to Israel's grievance? I don't think so, as hidden underneath these grumbles and moans are two sins of the heart that fuel God's anger. **Ungratefulness** for what God has provided and **unbelief** of what God has promised to provide.

Is complaining really that bad? Well, it clearly must be bad, as it evokes such an emotional reaction from God. Complaining is essentially two big sins rolled up and disguised as a small, more acceptable, minor transgression. Complaining is birthed in ungratefulness as well as entitlement, and if left to grow, it raises skepticism about whether God is truly in control, and finally matures into the inability to fully surrender to and trust in God. That is why God hates it!

We, too, may currently have many valid reasons to protest before God. The spiritual wilderness is a tough place. It is often unfair, unforgiving, and relentless. It is demoralizing, and even the most positive among us lose heart as we wander through it. Raising our grievances is a natural reaction that is completely logical and understandable. This is why this chapter is so important: our innate default tendency is to revert to this "cup is half empty" mentality and to complain. But God wants something different for us.

The origin of our complaints is in our ungrateful hearts. The Israelites complained because they were looking at what they lacked and what they wanted from God, no longer remembering what He had already done and provided. When we are ungrateful, we are telling God that all He has done was in vain and not good enough; we complain because He has failed to meet our expectations of what we believe we are entitled to.

146

Complaining also diminishes God. What we are effectively doing is saying that our circumstances and our problems are bigger than God. It is hopeless, and God cannot overcome our problems. God is angered because, despite all that He has done, we still lack faith in what He can do. We complain because it is easier to do that than to believe.

What, then, is the cure for this natural tendency to complain? What, then, is the antidote to this certain failure of an ungrateful and unbelieving heart? The answer is a "Honey-do" list, well, sort of.

If you are anything like my wife, then you always have things that need to be done around the house. If you are anything like me, then there is always another day to get it done. The net effect of these two extremes is an unhappy wife who resorts to complaining until I act. A bumper sticker I once read is so true for us, "When your husband says he will do something, it means he will do it; there is no need to remind him every six months." Enter my marriage-saving "Honey-do" list.

The idea was that Brenda would add everything that I needed to get done around the house to this list on the refrigerator, and I would mark them off as I completed them. This would keep me focused on the tasks that needed to be completed. Now, in truth, my intention with this "Honey-do" list was not really to remember all the things I needed to do. I needed no reminder that the kitchen cupboard door was hanging on one hinge and needed fixing as I opened that very cupboard daily. The real reason I proposed this list was so that we could keep track of everything I had already done, in truth, a "Honey-I've-done-it" list, if you will.

My logic was that if she could be reminded of all the tasks I had already completed around the house for her, she would moan less about the things I still had not got around to. Genius, I know. However, she is too smart and caught on quickly, the result is that we no longer have a "Honey-do" list on the refrigerator. I still take forever to get things done. Brenda still has to lovingly remind me that the trash won't walk itself out the door.

The point I am trying to make here is that the best way for us to stop the inevitable slide to chronic complaining is to "Remember" and then to "Repent." We need to remember what God has already done. We need to remember the price that Christ paid on Calvary. We need to remember that we have been liberated from the bondage of sin. We need to remember that this wilderness is part of God's plan for us, and He has led us here to prepare us to enter the Promised Land and equip us for the battles we are to face.

We then need to repent that we are so prone to forget and so prone to lose hope and faith in a God who can and will do abundantly more than you can ever imagine or dream of.

Go on then, don't be like Joel and Brenda. Do the smart thing. Draw up your "God-has-already-done-it" list to help you remember.

Day 29: **Oh Christmas Tree, Oh Christmas Tree**

The only Christmas trees we ever knew as children in South Africa were the artificial ones that came in a box, but that didn't stop us from decorating them in all their splendor. I am one of the fortunate guys who married a slightly "over-the-top" Christmas enthusiast. There is no such thing as over-decorating, and you will be excused if you ever visit our house during the holidays and mistakenly believe that you have arrived at the North Pole.

A couple of years after moving to the States, Brenda convinced me that it was an absolute necessity to have a real tree. This was cause for great excitement as we would finally get to do Christmas the same way they do it in the movies. We packed the kids in the car and drove off to pick out a tree. Just as in every Hallmark Christmas movie, we tied the tree to the top of the car and drove home singing Jingle Bells. I must concede that this remains one of my favorite Christmas memories, but cleaning up this mess in mid-January ranks up there with the worst.

Although I am still not sold on having a tree in every room, I do enjoy the festive season, and I love a pretty Christmas tree, too. There is something magical about a beautifully decorated tree with all the lights, the baubles, and the tinsel.

But alas, the thing about Christmas trees is that although they are pretty to look at, they don't bear any fruit. Similarly, I believe that is the problem with most of us Christians, too: pretty on the outside but completely barren with no fruit.

> *But the Holy Spirit produces this kind of fruit in our lives: Love, Joy, Peace, Patience, Kindness, Goodness, Faithfulness, Gentleness and Self-Control.* - Galatians 5:22-23 (NLT)

This verse is not complicated; if you have the Holy Spirit, then you will have the fruit. It is important not to confuse these with the gifts of the Spirit, which are only given to some. The Fruit of the Spirit is given to everyone who has surrendered themselves to the Spirit. So, the glaring question that arises is... Are we bearing fruit or not?

This is where we are so often deceived. Looking at the list above, we may claim to have some measure of this fruit in our lives. We do love people, we are generally kind, and we always have joy except when we are stuck in traffic. We show patience, provided the kids just do as we say, and although we may not have lacked self-control in college, we've pretty much mastered that now. So clearly, we must have the fruit of the spirit in our lives or, at the very least, a certain measure of it, right? Hmmm...not exactly.

To understand what Paul means by the fruit that the Holy Spirit produces, we need to separate what is of us and what is of the Spirit. Our natural temperament or character traits are what we bring to the table and should not be confused with what the Spirit produces. For example, I am by nature a gentle person, I am faithful, and I have loads of patience, but these are essentially innate. I was born with these. To put it in another way, I know many non-Christians who are still peaceful, joyful, gentle, and kind.

The Fruit of the Spirit is that which is over and above our natural character. It is a love greater than that which is of ourselves; it is a joy and peace that goes way beyond what is inherently already in us. The fruit that the Spirit produces is supernatural. It is not merely loving your family but being able to love your enemy and being willing to sacrifice everything for those who hate you. It is being kind and gentle not just to those who have been good to us but to those who are undeserving of any kindness and gentleness. When the Spirit abides in us, we are emptied and become a vessel that carries a higher love, peace, and kindness. Fruit that is far greater than that which we can muster on our own.

So, that question again... Are we bearing any fruit of the Spirit? Or are we Christmas trees?

A Christmas tree Christian is decorated with wonderful deeds and beautiful Christian virtues. They are good people with good intentions and, from the outside, look perfect. They attend church and even volunteer their time and money to worthy causes. They twinkle and shine on the outside, but, in reality, they are barren and bear no fruit. Draped from head to toe in Christianity but going season after season after season without any fruit?

> *I am the true vine, and my Father is the gardener. He cuts off every branch in me that bears no fruit, while every branch that does bear fruit he prunes so that it will be even more fruitful... No branch can bear fruit by itself; it must remain in the vine. Neither can you bear fruit unless you remain in me. I am the vine; you are the branches. If you remain in me and I in you, you will bear much fruit; apart from me you can do nothing. If you do not remain in me, you are like a branch that is thrown away and withers; such branches are picked up, thrown into the fire and burned.* – John 15:1-6

Jesus makes it clear that bearing fruit is not optional. If we are in Christ, and Christ is in us, we will bear fruit. Not just some measure, but all the fruit of the Spirit. If we bear no fruit, we can do nothing. We are rebuked like the fig tree that was beautifully green but with no fruit and will wither away.

Is this why God has led us into the wilderness? Do we need to drop the baubles and the tinsel? Is this what we need to repent of?

A desert is naturally a barren place, and if you are currently wandering through it, you will probably be producing very little fruit. Do not despair; Christ has not given up on you. He diligently continues to work the soil around you, and when the time is right, he will prune you, but be warned, this may be the most difficult time for you.

By pruning, God the Father removes what is dead and unhealthy. He cuts us back; we are completely exposed for what we really are... A barren, ugly, fruitless tree. No Christmas lights or pretty baubles to distract from the truth. We are cut back to the bare branches, and everyone will see us at our lowest. I have been there. Everything was stripped away: my pride, my honor, and my self-worth. All of it was cut away, and I was left vulnerable before all my friends and enemies.

But God, in His infinite wisdom, knows that it is better for us to go through a season of being completely stripped than to go through our whole lives decorated as Christmas trees.

When this barren season passes, we will bud again and form new branches. He promises that we will be fruitful again, and those who witness and share in this fruit will see what Christ has done and praise Him.

Day 30: **Antivirus now loading...**

Even though computers are supposed to make our lives easier, when they are compromised with viruses and malware, things quickly become more complicated. I'm not an expert on computers, but I do know that firewalls and antivirus software need to be updated. Cyberattacks are inevitable, and you will regret neglecting to load the proper antivirus. I'm not really sure how all of this antivirus software functions or what constitutes a decent firewall, but I do have a question. How do antiviruses and firewalls differ from one another?

My initial assumption was that it was essentially the same thing, but there is a difference, and they have been created for different purposes. In short, a firewall is designed to protect your computer from outside threats that are trying to gain access to it, while antivirus software is designed to scan your computer for threats that already are on your computer's drives. At least, that is my very basic take on it.

So, what do computer antivirus software, firewall installation, wandering in the wilderness, and repentance have in common? Bear with me as I try and explain.

First, let us consider the Gospel we are proclaiming today. Does it carry the same power as that preached by the apostles in Acts? Do you think that over the ages, it may have been diluted or watered down? Is it kind of lukewarm, neither hot nor cold, just one of the many compartments in our busy lives? Is Jesus Christ the One in your life or merely one of the things in your life? As modern-day believers, we are born and raised in the faith and have had "the good news" handed down from generation to generation. Sadly, over time, in many cases, it seems to have been diluted into mere religion. No power, just doctrine. No life change, just theology. No love, just rituals.

The truth is that the version of Christianity that we may have all been "installed" with may be compromised. By clinging onto this diluted Christianity, Satan has us exactly where he wants us. Christians who have just enough Christianity to stop them from truly seeking Christ. This may be why we need the desert, for us to bury this flawed, handed-down, and diluted version of Christianity.

To build on the computer analogy, as Christians born into the faith, we have been installed with a type of Christian firewall program. It may initially be effective in protecting us from sin trying to enter our lives. However, it is only as strong as its weakest point, and sin eventually finds a crack to enter in. Satan will plant seeds of doubt, seeds of compromise, and seeds of worldly repentance into this firewall, and in time, this firewall becomes the weak form of resistance that we see in many Christians today, who stumble and fall at every hurdle.

Additionally, this firewall gives us a false sense of security. When we do manage to fend off Satan's advances with this firewall, we begin to believe that we can overcome sin by our very own strength. The devil delights in this and allows us these minor victories as he knows that the biggest threats are not those on the outside but are those that are already within us. Firewalls are designed to protect us from external threats and attacks, but what about the Trojan horses that have breached the firewall and now lie undetected within us?

We continue to comfort ourselves with the assumption that this firewall is enough; we neglect to upgrade it by investing in our relationship with Christ. Once upon a time we prayed a magic little prayer, so we are good now. Satan celebrates because as long as we keep on believing we are okay, as long as we keep believing we are "saved," we will not change, and he will continue to destroy us unchecked from within.

This firewall version of Christianity is clearly missing something. It needs an antivirus installed with it. The antivirus will seek out the sin within us and destroy it. This is the Holy Spirit. Only when we are loaded with the Holy Spirit are we able to shine light into the dark corners of our hearts and expose the hidden sin eroding us from within.

If we allow Christ to install the full version of Christianity in us, we get the firewall and the antivirus. We do not have to settle for this inherited, watered-down version. Without the Holy Spirit living in our hearts, we have already lost the war, even though we take pride in some minor moral victories over sin. So, have you been loaded with the antivirus, or are you waging your entire future on a quickly eroding firewall? Do not be led astray by a diluted gospel. Jesus says:

> *Not everyone who says to me, 'Lord, Lord,' will enter the kingdom of heaven, but only the one who does the will of my Father who is in heaven. Many will say to me on that day, 'Lord, Lord, did we not prophesy in your name and in your name drive out demons and in your name perform many miracles?' Then I will tell them plainly, I never knew you. Away from me, you evildoers!* – Matthew 7:21-23

> *I know your deeds, that you are neither cold nor hot. I wish you were either one or the other! So, because you are lukewarm—neither hot nor cold—I am about to spit you out of my mouth.* – Revelation 3:15-16

As I said before, many Christians today have just enough Christianity to keep them from truly seeking Christ and thus ensuring that they remain lost. Oh, how I wish we were either hot or cold.

As we end this important part of the journey dealing with repentance, my prayer is this. If you are clinging to a watered-down version of Christianity, let it go. If you are lost in the desert and do not know where to run to too, drop this "just enough" faith and run into the arms of Christ. May we be moved by His love for us. Let us lay down our lives at the foot of the Cross, repent, and surrender everything to Him.

Let us be brave enough to reinstall the true and complete Gospel of Christ in us. Ensuring that we have installed the full version, both the firewall and antivirus. Our lives depend on it.

Part 4: Revival

Have you found what you're looking for?

We have spent the last 30 days reflecting on the reasons for this desert season. We have also reaffirmed the truths that often fade when navigating these trying times, and finally, we have been urged to move to repentance as a response to the great love that we bear witness to. After all that hard reading, we can eventually get to the part we have all been looking forward to. Revival. This is what we all signed up for, right? When you picked up this book a month ago, I promised you revival, not just survival, so now it's time to deliver. I am sure you are eager to get to the point where you can say you are *Revived and Kickin'*.

In the late eighties, U2 had a huge hit, "I Still Haven't Found What I'm Looking For," where Bono describes how he has scaled the highest mountains and done some crazy things in search of the "you" at the beginning of the song. (I would encourage you to listen to this song again and take note of the lyrics, considering the wilderness that you are in.) In the end, he confesses his personal beliefs but admits that he still hasn't found what he is looking for. I would hate for you to have wandered through the desert and still end up not finding what you are looking for. So, hopefully, in the next ten days, you can find the revival that you are yearning for.

Before we start, we probably need to ponder the question... What exactly is revival? Some popular synonyms are a comeback, resurgence, renewal, and restoration. Whenever I think of this phrase revival, I am taken back to big white tents erected in the middle of town and charismatic preachers evangelizing and pleading with people to return to God. The buzz and excitement that these revival gatherings would initially garner would sadly soon wither, and everything would just return to normal.

That is not the revival that we are seeking, we are looking for something that will stand the test of time. Something that will alter the trajectory of our lives. The good news is that this was exactly the revival that God had planned for you when He led you into your desert season, the bad news is that the revival you are hoping for in the Promised Land may not be exactly what you are looking for.

Unfortunately, I can't promise that after you exit the wilderness, your revival will include a "blessed life" filled with health, wealth, and prosperity. What I can promise you is that this revival will change everything... It will change who you are, how you think, how you love, what matters, and why you live. Maybe this has taken the shine and glitz off the revival that you had been anticipating... but I hope not.

The truth is that from when Jesus stepped into our world, he always seemed to reframe and redefine what we thought we knew. He sought to turn our wisdom upside down and inside out, causing us to wonder if we actually know anything at all. Our time in the wilderness draws us nearer to Him and our thinking changes resulting in a changed life. The formula for revival is simple:

Renew + Render = Revive

The **renewing** of your mind plus the **rendering** of your heart results in the **revival** of your life.

Simply put, revival is the transformation of our lives by the changing of our thoughts and the yielding of our passions or hearts' desires. It is not just an overflow of emotions that have been whipped up by upbeat praise and worship, nor by sermons designed as sweet honey to our ears. It is the reformation of our thoughts to be able to see the world as Jesus sees it. True revival starts where we end.

Stop imitating the ideals and opinions of the culture around you, but be inwardly transformed by the Holy Spirit through a total reformation of how you think. This will empower you to discern God's will as you live a beautiful life, satisfying and perfect in his eyes. – Romans 12:2 (TPT)

Over the next ten days, I will show you how I needed to apply this formula to reframe what I thought I knew. Maybe it will help you to start thinking differently...

Day 31: All in or not in at all

Rethinking MY EVERYTHING?

Your "everything" may mean very different things, depending on what you're referring to when you say "everything." When I am having a rough day, and someone asks me how I'm doing, I may respond that everything is fine...when everything is clearly not fine. Maybe we have promised to do everything to make our spouses happy, but what we mean by "everything" and what they understand are two very different types of "everything."

The first thought I needed to renew was what "everything" meant to me. I have always had this tendency to try to negotiate "my everything" with God, like how much is everything exactly? The truth is that it doesn't matter how I try to broker "everything." What matters is how God sees it. For Him, you're either all-in or not in at all. There really is no road called Middle Road when it comes to God's definition of "everything," and if you are seeking true revival, you need to be all-in.

The Bible is full of people trying to negotiate their "everything" with God. Fortunately for us, God is patient and understanding and knows that some of us need some extra time in the wilderness before we are ready to put all our chips on the line and go all in. We need time to process and count the cost. This is not a bad thing, of course, provided you get to the point of giving it all. As many wise people have noted, there is a great cost to discipleship...Everything!

This thought may terrify you, but take heart, we are in good company. In his old age, as the apostle John reflects on what to include while penning his Gospel, he finds it important to introduce us to a pharisee called Nicodemus and his story of transformation.

Nicodemus was not just your average Pharisee preaching in the marketplace or the local synagogue. No, he had worked himself all the way to the top as he was also a member of the Jewish Sanhedrin. This was the top brass of the Jewish leadership. Members of the Sanhedrin were religious rock stars and celebs, revered and honored everywhere. If the selling of merchandise were a thing back then, I am sure that they would not keep up with the demand for Nicodemus No.7 replica jerseys.

Anyway, my point is that the Sanhedrin had religious authority as the holiest of men, and they had negotiated ruling power with Rome. Therefore, we know that Nicodemus was powerful, wealthy, revered, and most definitely very knowledgeable in Jewish Scripture and law. He was a professional Jew. However, despite this, he still had questions and doubts and was still not able to connect the dots.

In chapter 3 of his Gospel, John tells us about Nicodemus' nighttime visit with Jesus. Why at night? Well, presumably, as a high-profile Jewish leader and religious celeb, he really didn't want this visit to be public knowledge as he needed to protect his reputation. Also, there is some symbolism with the visit at night as Nicodemus is still spiritually in the dark. Despite being on the honor roll for all his religious studies, despite being a professional holy man, and being the best of the best, he is still in the dark. (This is highlighted as, at the end of this encounter, Jesus teaches about remaining in the darkness or moving into the light.)

Before Nicodemus can even ask any questions, Jesus knows the questions in his heart. Although Nicodemus is one of the most educated and knowledgeable men in all of Israel with sound doctrine, Jesus begins to break down everything Nicodemus thought he knew by renewing his mind.

Later in Chapter 7, we see that Jesus's popularity has started taking off, and people are starting to believe that He may be the Messiah that they have been waiting for. The Jewish leaders have a problem, and in a meeting of the Sanhedrin, after a failed attempt to arrest Jesus, they plot their next move. Nicodemus raises to challenge his peers on whether the law would allow them to convict someone without a hearing.

Nicodemus now puts his reputation at risk by standing up for Jesus. His colleagues are quick to oppose him and mock him for his defense of Jesus. He is embarrassed and silenced into submission. However, something is very clearly different from the man who had requested a secret evening meeting with Jesus. Could it be that he has begun to render his heart?

Following Jesus comes at a much greater cost for Nicodemus than for most, and he understands the cost. For him, it would cost everything, and that meant every single thing, not only all he had but all he was. Like us, he struggles with this and likely also finds himself negotiating "his everything" with God. But he soon discovers, as I hope we do too, that everything simply means being all-in or not in at all.

John's third and final mention of Nicodemus comes in chapter 19, just after Jesus had been crucified. Joseph of Arimathea and Nicodemus are the ones who bury the lifeless body of Christ when his disciples have been scattered. This big-time "scared to be seen in public with Jesus" Pharisee is the one carrying the broken and bloodied body of Jesus to the tomb.

A couple of things are critical to take note of here. Nicodemus was a Pharisee, a "holy" man, and touching a dead body would make him unclean in Jewish law... remember the story of the Good Samaritan.

What is happening here is that Nicodemus is taking all of his doctrine, his elevated status in the community, his honor, his name, and the ancient tradition he has diligently upheld and tossing all of it. He is no longer concerned about who is looking or what they are thinking. All of it is now worthless to him; this choice to associate with Jesus means he will never be able to return to what things were before. He has tallied the high cost of discipleship, which seems trivial in comparison to the love he has witnessed on the cross.

John also says that Nicodemus brought about seventy-five pounds of myrrh and aloes to embalm the body. This would have been a small fortune and would normally have been reserved for a king's burial. Nicodemus takes the wealth that he has amassed and uses it to cover the body of a convicted criminal. Nicodemus sees no more value in his worldly wealth. It is all worthless to him.

Nicodemus died with Christ when he buried him. It would cost him everything, but I think he finally understood Jesus' words from that nighttime visit ...You must be born again.

Interestingly, none of the other Gospel writers mention Nicodemus, but John refers to him on these three separate occasions. Why, then, does John need to do this? Perhaps he knows that Nicodemus's story is not that unique; perhaps he anticipates that you and I will also struggle with the concept of being all-in; perhaps he just wants to illustrate how Jesus begins by renewing Nicodemus' mind, then rendering his heart, and ultimately transforming his life. We can see how the Spirit moves Nicodemus from wandering in this spiritual wilderness to a true revival in Christ. An illustration of how...

Renew + Render = Revival.

For you and I, maybe revival starts by rethinking "our everything" and truly giving and yielding our hearts to live that truth. Maybe our first step should be to let Jesus answer one of the secret nighttime encounter questions that we may have in our hearts. "How much is everything?"

Then Jesus said to his disciples, "If you truly want to follow me, you should at once completely reject and disown your own life. And you must be willing to share my cross and experience it as your own as you continually surrender to my ways. For if you choose self-sacrifice and lose your lives for my glory, you will continually discover true life. But if you choose to keep your lives for yourselves, you will forfeit what you try to keep. For even if you were to gain all the wealth and power of this world—at the cost of your own life—what good would that be? And what could be more valuable to you than your own soul? – Matthew 16:24-26 (TPT)

Day 32: **Diamond Rush**

Rethinking MY SEARCH?

For most of us, the thought of diamonds is automatically associated with high-end jewelry stores, posh sales personnel, and glass cabinets filled with the most exquisite bling. We only picture the small boxes with pretty ribbons and happy tears when these are shared. However, in most cases, these precious little stones have traveled quite a journey before ending up on the high street.

The city of Kimberley in the Northern Cape province of South Africa may not have much significance to you, but in the late 1800s, it was at the center of the great diamond rush. The city is situated in a very barren part of the country with limited rainfall, cold winters, and scorching summers. Despite this very harsh environment, people flocked there from all over the world in search of shiny little pebbles that promised to change their entire lives. They left everything behind in pursuit of the hope of life-changing riches. For these fortune seekers, finding what they were looking for was not as simple as walking over to Tiffany's; their search would require them to risk everything.

Despite growing up in church and receiving every sacrament, I found myself still searching for something valuable. I was constantly seeking the real Jesus and the revival He promised, but what I discovered was that maybe the first step was rethinking my search. Maybe like these diamond miners, what we are looking for...true revival...will not be found in the comforts of our local church but rather in the discomfort of the desert.

I know this is going to make me very unpopular amongst many pastors, but what you are looking for is not wrapped up in a small box with pretty ribbons available every Sunday morning. Rather, it is found in the brokenness of an abuse shelter, in the hopelessness of a rehab clinic, in the consolation and prayers around a hospital bed, and in the anxiety and tears of a neighbor who has been crushed. Maybe the problem is not what we are searching for but rather where we are looking for it. Maybe our first step should be to rethink our search.

In many cases, the church we have created has become a death trap for unsuspecting followers of Jesus. I believe that God sent His son to replace both unbelief and religion. I am not saying you should not belong or connect to a church; what I am saying is that you should not go "shopping" at a church for this revival that you are looking for. Many of our churches are designed to keep us comfortable. The gospel is preached in a way that leaves us with a warm and fuzzy feeling, and congregations are too easily offended. We are surrounded by like-minded people, but "church" was never meant to be finding a place where we "belong," but rather going where Christ needs us.

The point is this... You can spend your life looking for Jesus in church and never find him. The revival you are looking for may evade you if you fail to rethink your search and change your heart.

The Gospel of Mark is action-packed from the start, with so much happening in Chapter 1, but I would like us to pause for some reflection from verses 21 to 26, where Jesus casts out an impure spirit from a man. We often read right over some very important details in this fast-paced Gospel. Jesus is in

Capernaum teaching at the synagogue on the Sabbath. Take note...He is not in some random marketplace or street corner teaching to whoever happens to be in the vicinity. To put it in today's context, He was preaching at the local church on Sunday morning.

Why is this detail important? This implies that those listening to Jesus were not a random crowd of inquisitive onlookers. His listeners that morning were good, law-abiding, God-fearing, God-loving synagogue regulars. The point that is often overlooked is that the evil-possessed man is not a random passerby. He is in church every Sunday. A man who is learning and spending time every week in Scripture, honestly seeking God and desiring to please Him.

He attends church, Sunday after Sunday, listening to great teachers, but this unclean spirit within him is never confronted, never challenged, and never uncomfortable. This spirit is very content in letting the man be religious and has no problem with him attending church. We are not told what this unclean spirit is...Lust? Envy? Offense? Pride? Anxiety? Success? That is not important, but what we need to see is that this unclean spirit is quite content in co-existing with the man's religious convictions.

Are we like this man? We regularly attend church despite carrying something impure in us and masking it. The truth is the devil may have us exactly where he wants us. Caught in a death trap called church. Perhaps we would be better off knowing we were lost in the world, yearning for a savior...

We read in Scripture that this morning at the synagogue, Jesus teaches with great authority and conviction. The unclean spirit in the man is confronted, and it must rise and fight to survive, so it forces the poor man to cry out... "What do you want from us, Jesus? You have come to destroy us."

These impure spirits in us will be forced to fight as they cannot co-exist with the Holy Spirit being poured into us. You will be offended and challenged by the true Gospel. We may presume that by handing over our tithes and offerings, we will get Christ in return; much like buying that diamond in a fancy store. We leave church having got our weekly fix, having sung our worship songs, and feeling re-energized after the motivational sermon, but nothing truly changes in our lives. There is no revival. The impure spirits that we referenced above continue residing in us, and they have no problem with us attending church. We become experts at concealing and hiding these spirits. The devil has you exactly where he wants you.

Satan is not threatened by us attending church; his only fear is that we become the church.

What if your pursuit of Christ looked more like that of those eighteenth-century diamond seekers than the consumer ways of this modern world? What if we all searched for Christ in the dust of everyday life rather than in glamorous cathedrals? What if seeking revival meant not just finding a church that suits us but rather daily seeking Him in broken spaces?

Understand that I am not opposed to the church, but its purpose should be to equip us to go out and be the hands and feet of Christ. We need to rethink our search and shift from our consumer mentality. If you think I am being a little tough on churches, just read what God says in the book of Amos.

> *I can't stand your religious meetings. I'm fed up with your conferences and conventions. I want nothing to do with your religion projects, your pretentious slogans and goals.*
>
> *I'm sick of your fund-raising schemes, your public relations and image making. I've had all I can take of your noisy ego-music.*
>
> *When was the last time you sang to me? Do you know what I want? I want justice—oceans of it. I want fairness—rivers of it.*
>
> *That's what I want. That's all I want. – Amos 5:21-24(MSG)*

God is only interested in our hearts and what we do with the Gospel once we drive out of the church parking lot. Stop searching for God in a building but rather become the vessel that carries Him into the world. It is all about risking everything we think is important to find the diamond we are looking for in the dirt.

So, here is the question...When we eventually pass through this desert season, do we just go back to the old status quo? Pick up where we left off, albeit bruised and battered, and go back to a life of Sunday morning praises and thirty-second graces... or has our mind been renewed, and are we willing to render our hearts to become the hands and feet of Christ? Search for Him where it is not comfortable, and maybe you, too, will find TRUE revival in the dirt...

Day 33: **In the Rearview Mirror**

Rethinking MY RESPONSE?

Life, they say, is all about choices. Not just the choices between different paths but, more importantly, how we choose to respond to what comes across our chosen path. Our response is what determines the trajectory of our whole lives and as we seek revival, we need to first rethink our response.

Now, we have already dedicated much time during the previous chapters of this book to reflecting on our response to our desert season. I would hope that you are much clearer as to the reasons why you have been led into the wilderness and that you are already responding to this season with much more hope. Today, however, I want us to consider how we will respond once we exit the desert and enter the Promised Land. I would like us to rethink our response to answered prayers.

Culture teaches us to never look back but rather to strife towards what lies ahead. There is no time to ponder what has gone on before, but we are geared to move forward. Always focusing on progress and where we are going. Now, I am not opposed to progression, but I do believe we would be wise to sometimes pause and consider what is in the rearview mirror. Allow me to rephrase a famous George Santayana quote, "Those who cannot remember the past are condemned to repeat it." Here is my twist on it: "Those who fail to remember the wilderness are condemned to end up there again." I am sure that extended regular desert excursions are not desirable at this point, correct?

What I wish to emphasize is this: I think it is imperative that as we ready ourselves to exit the spiritual wilderness and enter the Promised Land, we do not leave the lessons we learned behind but that we remember what God has done for us and how he has changed our hearts in the desert. We may be tempted to drive off into the sunset, forgetting about this season, but we should not be surprised if very soon you find ourselves wandering in the wilderness again.

As you glance into the rear-view mirror, your response is important. Do you forget the hard times you have been through and just move on to the next chapter in your life? Do you just check this off as a bad patch and proceed to bigger and better? Or, has this desert journey been so impactful that you can never go back to what you used to be?

In the Gospel of John, there are two very similar healing miracles separated by just a few chapters. The first is the account of the healing of the paralyzed man (Chapter 5), and the second details the healing of the blind man (Chapter 9). But why would John, who was trying to summarize the good news of Christ into a few short pages, detail two healing miracles that were so alike? John only included seven of Jesus' many miracles in his entire gospel, so why are these two essentially the same? Well, the answer lies not in their many similarities but rather in the one big difference between the two healing miracles; it is our key thought for today... Response. The key difference is the response to the miracle, and we are challenged to rethink our response to our miracles and answered prayers. This response is the difference between revival and mere survival.

So, let's start by looking at some of the similarities:

- both involve a miracle of healing

- both men have been waiting for a miracle for a very long time
- both miracles take place in Jerusalem, and both at a pool (the first at the pool of Bethesda and the other at the pool of Siloam)
- both miracles take place on the Sabbath

The difference, as stated, is found in what each man does with his miracle...They have both been praying and hoping for years that God intercede but what happens when they finally get their miracle? And more importantly, how does this choice or response impact the rest of their story?

The first man was lame and waiting at the pool of Bethesda to be healed. Tradition had it that an angel would come and stir the water and that whoever got into the pool first would be healed, but this man, being lame, could not get into the pool quick enough. This man's hope of healing was in the pool water; all he needed was someone to help him get into the pool first. Jesus tells him to pick up his mat and walk, bypassing the pool water in which the man has placed his hope. The man picks up his mat but does not bother looking in the rear-view mirror and just walks off. He has gotten his miracle, and now he can finally get back to living his life. Hallelujah! Now, I am sure that he was grateful for his miracle, and I do not wish to imply otherwise, but bear with me as I exaggerate and stretch the details to emphasize my point.

As he is walking away, some Jewish leaders confront him about carrying his mat on the Sabbath, and he defends himself by saying the guy who healed him told him to carry his mat. Seriously... Was he in such a hurry to get on with his life that he didn't bother to get the name of the guy who healed him?

Later, Jesus meets him at the temple, and knowing his heart, Jesus tells the man to turn from sin. The man must have taken offense at the rebuke, as he returns to the Jewish leaders to report that this man named Jesus is the one going around healing people on the Sabbath. Take note of the effect that the man's response has on the trajectory of his life. Though he received his miracle, he remained paralyzed in spirit, unable to do anything for God's kingdom.

The second man was born blind, and the fascinating part of the story is how Jesus heals him. Jesus spits into the dust on the ground and rubs the mud over the man's eyes. He sends this man to wash his eyes in the pool of Siloam, and here is the major difference between the two stories: John 9:7 says the man came back seeing. He came back.

He did not just carry on his merry way but checked his rear-view mirror and returned, testifying to his neighbors about what Jesus had done. As in the previous story, this man, too, is confronted by the Jewish leaders who try to frame Jesus as not being from God because he performs miracles on the Sabbath. The healed young man responds by questioning their reasoning and asking how a sinner can make the blind see.

As the man continues to talk about Jesus and the miracle he has received, we witness how his faith deepens. Initially, he refers to Jesus as a prophet; he then asks the Pharisees if they also want to become disciples of Jesus, thus implying that he is now a disciple; later, he boldly opposes the Pharisees by declaring that Jesus is from God. Finally, as he later meets up with Jesus and is asked, "Do you believe in the Son of Man?" his answer resonates to this day... "My Lord, I believe."

This man's initial response to "come back" directs the course of his entire life. The man has not only been healed from his physical blindness, but because he paused and returned to testify about his miracle, he was healed of his spiritual blindness, too. He sees Jesus as the Messiah and not just a prophet.

We have all prayed for miracles, for God to make a way out of this desert, but the question we need to answer is this... What are we going to do with our miracle?

Only you can answer that question for yourself, but I pray that you pause, look in your rear-view mirror, and return to testify of what Jesus has done. In doing this, we receive much more than just a miracle; we are healed from our spiritual blindness.

Perhaps God has led us into this desert to heal us from blindness, to lead us to a new life, revived and kickin' so that we can see Jesus for who he truly is and can testify with our entire being... "Jesus, my Lord, I believe."

Day 34: **Made in China**

Rethinking MY RULES?

Growing up, we are taught to obey the rules and do what is right. That is good advice, generally, but the problem with our "right" is that it could be completely wrong. My desert season has been a time for me to reconsider what I define as right, a safe place to rethink my rules. The truth is that I was never going to get anywhere with my rules, but I held on to them like they were my salvation. Jesus became extremely unpopular with those who made a living by keeping the rules because he constantly invited his listeners to reconsider their rules. We receive that same invitation today; you see, it isn't about what we do or don't do, but about what He has already done. The issue with our rules is that we have no trouble applying them rigorously to others, but when it comes to applying them to ourselves, we tend to always look for ways to get around them. Remember when we spoke earlier about using Christ's light as a flashlight?

Some time ago I watched the movie "Wonder" starring Julia Roberts. I cried my eyes out and was a complete mess right through the movie, but there was one line that I have never forgotten and remains so impactful in my decision-making:

"When given the choice between being right and being kind. Choose kind."

Wait, what? There's a choice? Shouldn't we always strive to do the "right" thing? I love this quote so much because somewhere in this lies a core Christian value, but allow me to adapt it to make this clearer:

"When you are faced with a choice between right and love. Choose love."

I am not saying go out and break all the rules or throw away the rulebook; rather, we should put them in their correct place, beneath love. Love first. If you are struggling with this, don't despair; the New Testament is full of people wanting to default back to the rulebook. It is easier to abide by the rules than to love. We must comprehend that enforcing rules upon people will not get them to heaven, but if we can choose love, there is a greater possibility that they will choose right. This applies to our children, peers, and anyone who crosses our path.

Jesus took all these rules and bundled them up into only one commandment. Love one another. Let me put it another way, "Never let the love of the law replace the law of love." Your rules are good, but Christ's love is great. So, rethink your rules and choose love every time.

Now, I know what some of you are thinking. What on earth does all this have to do with China? I once had to take a business trip to China, so I sat my little girls down to tell them that I would be away for a few nights. Kiki, my eldest, had a quick response, "Oh, China, yeah, I know where that is." I was a little taken aback, but before I could answer, she explained, "It's where they make everything." How did she know that was my question? "Because all the tags say so, Daddy," she confidently answered.

I remember this conversation whenever I see a "Made in China" tag or label. A tag not only confirms the product's origin but also infers so much more from it. What does your tag say? Made Orthodox, made Catholic, maybe it reads strictly Reformed, or simply Evangelical. Here is what it should say,

"Made in Christ." The only tag that you should ever carry is the Cross. Love should be your tag. When the world reads this tag, it should leave them in no doubt. The world will know we are Christians because of our love.

"We love because He first loved us." – 1 John 4:19

The idea is not to go crazy and have "Made in Christ" t-shirts printed, we should rather be rethinking our rules and rendering our hearts to choose love. This love is the label that the world will see. How do I know this? Because Jesus said so:

> *A new command I give you: Love one another. As I have loved you, so you must love one another. By this everyone will know that you are my disciples, if you have love one another* – John 13:34-35

Your words don't tell me who you are. Your deeds and works may still leave me wondering and questioning what lies underneath. The only way I know for sure is by checking your tag. Do you have "love for one another"? That's when you are "Made in Christ." Scripture is again very clear on the fact that without love, everything we do is just noise:

> *If I speak in the tongues of men or of angels, but do not have love, I am only a resounding gong or a clanging cymbal. If I have the gift of prophecy and can fathom all mysteries and all knowledge, and if I have a faith that can move mountains, but do not have love, I am nothing. If I give all I possess to the poor and give over my body to hardship that I may boast, but do not have love, I gain nothing.* – 1 Corinthians 13:1-3

The purpose of the deserts that we are led into is not mere survival, learning a lesson, and recommitting to the law or set of rules. This law won't save you. Remember, it is not about what we do but what has already been done in Christ. We are not going through these tough trials so that we can become better "keepers of the rules"; what God seeks is the rendering and yielding of your heart. Then, you begin to experience true revival. Not a revival that comes from keeping the rules but a revival and freedom that comes from choosing love over the rules.

Day 35: If it ain't broke, it probably needs fixin'

Rethinking MY VIEWS?

Right through the Gospel, Jesus always shows up and flips the script. He not only turns over the money trader's tables in the temple but does the exact same thing with everything we think we know. Very often, this includes the things that we are so certain of and our views that are so deeply embedded. Jesus often challenges us to rethink our views and to question what we think we know, and as you may already have discovered, there is no better place for doing this than in the wilderness.

As a perennial procrastinator, one of my go-to excuses when trying to get out of a task is, "If it ain't broke, don't fix it." Much to my wife's frustration, I pretty much wait until something falls apart before I reluctantly move to repair it. Now, in many cases, constant tinkering with something that is working fine is probably a bad idea, and you may be well advised to heed my words of wisdom, but when it comes to your faith, the opposite rings true. As far as your inherited faith, preconceived views, and religious opinions go, if it ain't broke, then it probably needs fixin'. You see, there are too many Christians today who believe that their faith is working just fine, but in truth, it is in desperate need of fixing.

The outline of Mark's Gospel shows us how the disciples are forced to rethink their presuppositions and ideas about the Messiah. As young Jewish men, everything they had been taught while diligently studying the Torah and everything they had been anticipating and waiting for concerning the coming Messiah was about to be flipped upside down. Their Savior and His salvation plan for Israel would be completely different from the narrative they had been fed by those in the know. What is even more insightful is that this revelation comes at a pivotal moment right in the middle of the Gospel (Mark 8:31) and is in response to Jesus' simple question, "Who do you say I am?"

Before this, Mark portrays how Jesus goes about showing his followers that He is the Messiah by illustrating His authority in words and deeds. Once Peter answers this pivotal question, "Who do you say I am?" and recognizes Jesus as the Messiah, the narrative changes to break down and disassemble the views and ideas of what they believed the Messiah would be (their preconceived idea of conquering warrior Messiah) in contrast to what Jesus truly wanted them to see, the Messiah as a servant of the Lord. The disciples are forced to rethink their understanding of the Messiah and turn their focus toward the Cross, the purpose of the Messiah.

Growing up in a Christian home, I learned all about Jesus and his miracles and never questioned His authority. In the process, I "gave" my heart to the Lord as I was petrified of the alternative of going to hell... But the turning point for me, as it was for Peter, was recognizing and being able to confess that Jesus truly is the Christ; He is the Messiah! This is the pivot; this is where everything turns.

Our time in the wilderness is meant to open our eyes to Christ's authority by experiencing His provision and grace during our trials, allowing us to answer Jesus' simple question, "Who do you say I am?" Once we confess this... Jesus begins the process of breaking down our preconceived and fabricated ideas of Him and Christianity. We are forced to rethink our views. We begin to understand and model ourselves around what He showed us, not what we were taught.

So, what does this look like? We are called to joyfully suffer in serving others so that they can be encouraged by our hope and peace despite our current heartache and trials. In addition, we are called to adopt a servant mindset that seeks to jump to the back of the line and is always looking to put others' needs and desires first—a suffering servant as modeled by Christ.

Some of you may recall those WWJD bracelets that reminded us to ask, "What Would Jesus Do?" Well, we don't need to question any longer because Jesus has already given us the answer,

"For even the Son of Man did not come to be served but to serve, and to give His life as a ransom for many." – Mark 10:45

The answer is a servant mindset, even if it means giving up our own life, dreams, and desires. The apostle Paul further emphasizes what the mindset of a Christ follower should be and calls us to rethink our views and current mindset.

> *Be free from pride-filled opinions, for they will only harm your cherished unity. Don't allow self-promotion to hide in your hearts, but in authentic humility, put others first and view others as more important than yourselves. Abandon every display of selfishness. Possess a greater concern for what matters to others instead of your own interests. And consider the example that Jesus, the Anointed One, has set before us. Let his mindset become your motivation...he emptied himself of his outward glory by reducing himself to the form of a lowly servant.* – Philippians 2:3-5,7

We need a change in our thinking, a new mindset, the mindset of Christ as he illustrates a servant's heart by washing his students' feet while they are bickering about where they rank and who gets the seat next to Him. As they are jostling for position, he takes the place of the lowest among them. The only way you can yield a servant's heart as Christ did is by starting with a servant's mindset. You are what you think, I guess?

Many of us believe we are okay; we don't need fixin'. We have our golden ticket into heaven because we once said this magic prayer, and we practice some religious rituals or customs that cover up what is really going on inside. We may think we are not broke, but we desperately need fixin'. Our mindset and views are set on ourselves; in the end, if we are honest, it is all about ourselves. We believe because, in return, we get to go to Heaven. We serve at church because it makes us look holy and pious, but our hearts and our heads are merely concerned with self.

This is why I need the desert, this is why you need the desert...to change our thinking and our mindset, to instill a servant mindset, to fix what we believe ain't broke.

Day 36: Time to change your beatitude?

Rethinking MY HURT?

They say that your attitude determines your altitude; in other words, a good positive attitude will result in you reaching greater heights. I can't argue with that, but even though those words are great for a team pep talk, they fall flat for the person at the end of their rope. When you have been handed a truckload of lemons and your faith and hope lie in ruin, finding a positive attitude to reach new heights is easier said than done.

On the morning of Jesus's sermon on the mount, I wonder what was on his mind as he made his way through the large crowds to the top of that small hill. As he prepared to give the greatest sermon ever, how would he captivate their attention? Certainly, they had come to see miracles, so a couple of miraculous healings should do the trick. Perhaps a few words of thunder from the onset would set the right tone and ensure that they came to repentance by the hundreds.

Jesus looks around at the thousands gathered and sees straight into the eyes of each one; he sees the broken, the hurting, the desolate, the persecuted, the weak sinners, the ill, the hungry, and those who are there because they have lost all hope, they no longer know what to believe in and their faith is crumbling as the God of their forefathers has been silent for four hundred years. They are a nation oppressed under Roman rule and taxes; their religious and political leaders have sold out to protect their own interests as they desperately cling to hold on to their vassal powers granted by Rome. Israel is broken. Israel is hurting. Jesus starts his sermon on the mount by asking the crowd to rethink their hurt. Jesus wants them to see their pain in a new way...with a Kingdom view.

No doubt, as you switch through your news channels or scroll through your feed, you see what Jesus saw when he looked into the crowd that day. Brokenness. Hopelessness. Pain. Hurt. Fear and anxiety. A faith crisis. Maybe the wilderness has brought you to your knees. You feel that there is no way out. Jesus has the same message for each one of us. We should rethink our hurt by taking encouragement from the beatitudes. These eight upside-down phrases that Jesus quotes as an introduction to his sermon on the mount (Matthew 5) are what Jesus uses to connect with his broken audience and what I believe he uses to connect with our hurting world today and with each of us amid our pain.

For a long time, I read the beatitudes as conditional statements. In other words, if I wanted to get into the Kingdom of Heaven, then I needed to become poor in spirit. If I wanted to inherit the earth, I needed to show a meek and gentle nature. This is not what Jesus is saying; remember, his blood is enough. He paid it all; there is nothing that you need to do. What he is trying to communicate is this: blessed are the broken because they can be sure that their brokenness is temporary, and they can have divine joy now in the knowledge that the Kingdom is already here.

Religion tells us happy and blessed are those who have worked it all out, have the right answers, have not strayed, and have kept the faith...Those will go to Heaven. Jesus looks into the crowd and perhaps sees one young woman who has lost her faith and hope; for her, God was silent when she pleaded for help. Perhaps she has given up on God. Jesus looks into her eyes, sees her pain and doubt, and says, "Blessed be the poor in spirit, for theirs is the kingdom of heaven." In the same way, Jesus looks at us and says, my kingdom has already come, and therefore, you have a reason for great joy even though your world is falling apart and you have lost your faith, your hope, and your way. You can still be happy.

Our culture tells us that the blessed are the successful. They will be praised and exalted. Blessed are the strong who will do whatever it takes to win; the reward is the blessing of abundance and wealth. Jesus looks into the crowd, and perhaps his eyes meet that of a father who had just lost his livelihood. He has failed; he has lost everything despite working around the clock (including the Sabbath) to try and make ends meet. Jesus says to him, "Blessed are those who mourn, for they will be comforted. Blessed are the meek, for they will inherit the earth." Even though you are despondent and have lost everything, even if you have made some mistakes and now are filled with regret, even if you feel you are weak and there is no fight left in you, do not mourn but take divine joy because Jesus has already come and he will provide you everything on the earth that you need. Be happy and encouraged; He has got you covered.

Sometimes, it feels like those who cheat and steal often win in life at the expense of those who try to do what's right. The ones who have no mercy always seem to get ahead. We are taught to be ruthless in business and take no prisoners. Jesus looks at the sea of faces in front of him and sees the man who tried to pursue what is right but is still empty and has a void that can't be filled; he sees the widow who takes pity on the desperate and shows mercy but struggles with the anxiety of not knowing where her children's next meal will come from. Jesus notices the couple who are broken because even though they were pure in heart and had the best intentions, the marriage is hell on earth. Jesus looks around and sees so many who are just trying to keep the peace, even if it means constantly taking the back seat.

There is so much brokenness and so much hurt, and Jesus turns to them and says, "Blessed are those who hunger and thirst for righteousness, for they will be filled. Blessed are the merciful, for they will be shown mercy. Blessed are the pure in heart, for they will see God. Blessed are the peacemakers, for they will be called children of God. Blessed are those who are persecuted because of righteousness, for theirs is the kingdom of heaven."

As you come to the end of your desert journey, I can't promise you that all your hurt will disappear, but I challenge you to rethink your hurt. What if you had a different attitude, or beatitude, to your hurt and brokenness? Today, Jesus forgets the ninety-nine around you and looks straight into your eyes... He sees your pain, He sees your hurt, He knows how broken you really are... and perhaps these words are just for you:

Blessed are the broken-hearted and those who are hurting, because they will feel less broken when they see their hurt in light of the joy they have received in Christ.

Day 37: **Quit trying and start dying!**

Rethinking MY EFFORT?

Occasionally, when we attempt to articulate our thoughts, the words we choose may leave our listeners more perplexed than informed. They may even think that we've lost our minds. This next chapter is especially for my mother as I hope to explain a phrase that I dropped during one of our conversations about faith. On reflection, I understand why it may have had her scrambling for the hotline number, worried that I was about to harm myself.

I can't remember all the details of this conversation, but I recall that I was working through some doubts and struggles at that time. As an empathetic mom, she listened and tried to encourage me by reassuring me that though we may sometimes fail as Christians, we should always just try and do better. I lost it and yelled back… "I am sick of this! We should all just quit trying and start dying!" What I thought was a great theological eureka moment was, however, not quite as enthusiastically received by my mother, whose anxious expression clearly showed that she had heard something completely different from what I had meant to say.

Even though I see the humorous side now, the point I was trying to convey was that, as Christians, we should stop trying to be better and do better. We should quit trying to avoid temptation and sin through our own efforts, and we should stop spending all our energy and willpower trying to be "good" when, by nature, we are rotten to the core. On the contrary, we should rather be "dying to self", as directed by Scripture:

> *Then Jesus said to his disciples, "If you truly want to follow me, you should at once completely reject and disown your own life. And you must be willing to share my Cross and experience it as your own as you continually surrender to my ways.* – Matthew 16:24 (TPT)

Sharing his Cross means us "dying to self" and surrendering to his ways. We no longer seek our own ways and do not need to harness our best efforts to be "good" enough.

The apostle Paul had a deeply profound understanding of this, and in his letter to the Galatians, he emphasizes this point in my favorite verse:

> *My old self has been crucified with Christ. It is no longer I who live, but Christ lives in me. So, I live in this earthly body by trusting in the Son of God, who loved me and gave himself for me.* – Galatians 2:20 (NLT)

In the desert, we are called to rethink our efforts, as our efforts will not bring us closer to God. It is only when you reach the end of your effort, that God can start. While you keep trying, God remains on the sidelines waiting to be subbed on. Our efforts may be exactly what is tripping us up. We desperately need to quit trying and start dying.

In the Gospel of Luke, we find the parable commonly known as the parable of the prodigal son. I dislike this title as it directs all our emphasis to the younger brother and the error of his ways, but in truth, this parable is about so much more. If I had my way, I would title it. "The parable of the loving father, the prodigal son, and the lost son." With this "new title" in mind, I would encourage you to read the parable in Luke 15 together with the two preceding parables of the lost sheep and the lost coin, as these parables should be read as a unit.

The core message here centers around that which is lost and how important the "lost one" is to God. The importance of the one is clearly illustrated by how it progresses from one in a hundred sheep, then to one in ten coins, and finally to one of two sons. However, the question that I would like us to ponder is this... Is the prodigal son, perhaps not the lost son after all?

Maybe the best place to start is by defining the word "prodigal," which generally means extravagantly wasteful. There is no doubt that the younger son was extravagantly wasteful as he burned through half of his father's wealth in such a short space of time. Unfortunately, he must own this title. This son, however, repents and returns to the father, who rejoices at his return. Up to this point, this parable runs parallel to the other two parables of The Lost Sheep and the Lost Coin. The lost has been found, and therefore, there is now great rejoicing.

If this story was just about the younger brother, then the parable could have ended at this point, and we would still have had a great parable. But our attention is now diverted to the older brother, the "good" son who was _trying_ to do everything right.

Both sons are lost – the one who left home (like the sheep that was lost) and the one who was lost even while at home (like the coin). The difference is that the prodigal younger brother was lost but is subsequently found, and this is celebrated. The older brother has not been prodigal and has not left home, but he remains lost, and the father has no reason to celebrate, not even with a small goat, until the older son is found.

When the younger brother's world comes crashing down, he finds himself amongst the pigs. He realizes who he truly is without the father and at this moment "dies to self", he is broken and is now willing to become a servant. By returning home and willingly placing himself under his father's dominion, he is no longer lost. He has been saved and there is reason for great celebration.

On the other hand, the older brother gets an A+ for effort. He does everything right and tries to please the father in every single way, but the father finds no reason to celebrate as his son remains lost. This parable leaves us a little uneasy and perplexed. We all want the good guy to win, but in this case, he doesn't. We want the guy who has worked the hardest and tried his best to get the prize, but here, he doesn't. Jesus wants you to rethink your effort. To be clear, I am not advocating being prodigal and wasteful, but what is important is to comprehend that trying to be good enough will not win you the prize. This only happens when you "die to self."

These parables tell us about a shepherd who leaves the ninety-nine sheep and seeks out the lost one. They tell us about a woman who leaves her nine coins to search for her lost coin. In the third parable, however, the father stays at home and does not go out in search of his prodigal son. Why is that? Why would he not do what the shepherd and the women did and go in search of that which was lost? Well, maybe the father sees something that we had initially missed. Maybe he knows that Junior, although wasteful, will eventually return when the money dries up, and maybe he decides to stay home and seek the older son, who is lost despite never leaving. The story ends with the father leaving the joyous celebration of the prodigal son's return in search of his son, who remains lost.

You could be attending church religiously every week and doing a bunch of good Christian deeds. You may have an A+ for all your efforts, but that does not mean you are not lost. Unless we see ourselves as unworthy, we cannot possibly fall upon the grace of God. Unless we realize that we are spiritually destitute, and unless we see ourselves and our best efforts as only good enough to end up amongst the pigs, we will never experience revival despite our good works and church attendance. It is only the needy and the broken who reach out for help or who need saving.

Maybe, like the older brother, we need to rethink our efforts; they cannot save us and will not make us good with God. Only the Cross can do that, and you need to crucify your old self on the Cross. So, let us stop trying to do better and be better; instead, let's consider death on the Cross. Is it not time that you quit trying and start dying?

Day 38: Rewrapping your Gift

Rethinking MY CALLING?

Some of the most precious memories that I have as a parent are having witnessed my children's joy and thrill on Christmas mornings. I fondly recall lying in bed listening to the girls nervously making their way down the stairs, hoping that little Elfie was kind enough to give Santa a good report. I wait and listen, just a few more seconds...and then, this moment of nervous silence quickly turns to laughter and a burst of joy as they rush upstairs, "Wake up! Wake up! Mommy, Daddy! Wake up! Santa was here! Santa came!".

A couple of years back, this was exactly how I was dragged out of bed to come and behold the Christmas bounty that was lying under the tree. Once the excitement of opening the presents had subsided and I had helped myself to the rest of Santa's half-eaten cookies that he had so kindly left for me, I noticed my girls doing something very odd. They started rewrapping the Christmas presents.

I watched as they placed their "rewrapped" gifts under the tree and gathered their dolls in a semi-circle around the tree. They proceeded to relive and enjoy the excitement and joy of Christmas morning again and again by handing the rewrapped gifts to their dolls to open, never wanting the moment to end.

Many of us are just like my girls on Christmas morning. In life, we have experienced great joy and received wonderful gifts, but we do not want our Christmas morning to end. Perhaps we have been called to do something great with our gift, but we instead choose to rewrap it and relive the joy of opening it again and again instead of experiencing the true fulfillment that it can bring when we actually use it.

Why are you here? What is your purpose? What is God calling you to? These questions are amplified during our desert seasons. How do we know, for sure, what God wants us to do? I can't answer that for you, but what I do know is this: God wants us to rethink our calling and our purpose. The plan is not that we find Jesus and keep him wrapped under the tree.

It is hard for me to add anything new when it comes to finding your purpose and answering your call, as many who are much wiser than me have written extensively on these topics. However, I do believe that as God called me to rethink my calling, three points stood out very clearly that I would like to share with you.

Firstly, maybe it is not about me. This is also the opening thought of Rick Warren's best-seller, *The Purpose Driven Life*, and as he once commented, he could have stopped writing after this opening line. Perhaps we have been given a gift just to share it? I knew that my calling would always be tied to His Kingdom, but what did that actually mean, and where was the starting point? I found the answer in the bridge of one of my favorite songs:

> *Heal my heart and make it clean,*
>
> *open up my eyes to the things unseen,*
>
> *Show me how to love like you have loved me.*
>
> *Break my heart for what breaks yours,*
>
> *Everything I am for Your Kingdom's cause...*
>
> (Lyrics to Hosanna by Hillsong United)

So, maybe the correct question is not what is my purpose or what is God calling me to do...but rather, what breaks His heart? Of course, there are many answers to that question, but your purpose is probably found where what breaks God's heart meets with what breaks your heart. Maybe that is the starting point when rethinking our calling.

My heart is broken by how cheap we have made grace. God witnessed His only Son being nailed to a cross; He experienced the anguish of having his child cry out to Him while dying, knowing this was the only way to save each of us. In the end, only to witness us settle for a diluted and corrupted version of faith. This breaks God's heart, and it breaks mine too.

Secondly, comfort and purpose don't mix. I always thought that my calling would somehow go hand-in-hand with my talents, but I soon realized that my calling was much bigger than anything I could bring to the table. Your talents and your gifts should certainly be used to God's glory, but your calling will most definitely be something that you cannot do on your own. God likes using our weaknesses and not our talents when performing the miraculous.

The safe option is to do what comes naturally or what you are good at and comfortable with. The "God" option is to do what is impossible. I pray we have the courage and faith to always go with the God option and choose the impossible.

Thirdly, our past cannot disqualify or qualify us! Remember, this has nothing to do with you or me... God is not a god of coincidence and chance; you have not walked the specific path of your life by accident. I believe that God, like a grandmaster in chess, has meticulously planned for you to be exactly where you are at this given time for His specific purpose...

The book of Esther in the Old Testament tells us about a young Jewish girl who defies all the odds to eventually become the queen of the most powerful empire in the world when she is chosen by the king of Persia. There is a plot to murder the entire Jewish nation, and her stepfather pleads with her to use her position to save Israel. Afraid to approach the king, as an unsolicited approach of the King was punishable by death, she fasts for three days before confessing to him that she is a Jew and pleading for her people. Israel is saved, and the rest, as they say, is history.

It is easy for us to acknowledge Esther as the hero that she turns out to be, but much like us, this girl had some serious baggage. She was hardly a model young Jewish girl.

- She mixed with and married into the faith of the pagans, which was forbidden by the law.
- She lied about her faith and did not tell anyone about her Jewish roots, which means that she was not practicing her Jewish faith.
- Lastly, she may have been a bit more obsessed with her external beauty than her internal relationship with God, as evidenced by her strictly following the protocol of "beautifying" herself for a whole year in preparation for meeting the king with the goal of physically and sexually pleasing him when she would be brought before him.

I am not here to get into Esther's missteps; trust me I have enough of my own to keep me occupied, but she was willing to risk everything she had "worked" for to save a nation that no longer viewed her as one of theirs... and because of this, God was able to use her despite her imperfections and to deliberately position her. Her stepfather beautifully reminds her of this with this famous verse:

If you keep quiet at this time, deliverance and relief for the Jews will arise from some other place, but you and your relatives will die. Who knows if perhaps you were made queen for just such a time as this? - Esther: 4:14 (NLT)

Who knows if you have been made king of your castle for just such a time as this? What is it that God is calling you to do, and what breaks your heart as well as His heart? Like Esther, maybe we come from the wrong stock, or our tainted history has already disqualified us, maybe the impossible seems too hard, or perhaps we are reluctant to let go of everything we've "worked" for to position ourselves.

Despite all of this, are we willing to take the gift of Jesus that we have received and follow God's call, or are we just going to rewrap it and place it back under the tree to reopen and enjoy every Sunday morning?

Day 39: **Life's a Foxtrot**

Rethinking MY HUSTLE?

Quick, Quick, Slow... Slow... Quick, Quick, Slow... Slow... Be sure to keep the count, and the rest will be easy to remember.

I am no ballroom dancer (though I secretly wish I was), and you would be foolish to take any ballroom dancing tips from me. The truth is that the sum of all my ballroom dancing expertise is limited to that which I have gathered while watching a couple of episodes of "Dancing with the Stars!" But I do know that keeping count is imperative. Keep missing a beat, and you'll end up watching from the sidelines.

When I think about it, I believe life is very similar to that of a foxtrot. There are times when things are rushed, and we need to go quick, quick...but then we need to deliberately step back and go slow, slow. If not, we will miss the beat, and we could end up on the floor. The world we live in today seems to have lost count, too; it is more like Quick, Quick, Quicker... Quick, Quick, come on, get moving or get out of the way!!! I am sure we can all relate to this, but this is not what God wants for us. The Bible consistently instructs us to be still, to stop and listen, and to retreat to a quiet place. If we fail to do this, we can expect things to start falling apart.

As we seek revival, a crucial step is to rethink our hustle. What does that mean? What are we chasing? Why the unceasing hurry? Things to do, people to see, and crammed calendars. No wonder we are all so stressed and wound up, with no margin left in our schedules. It is not just our lives that are too busy; our minds are overloaded and unable to process all the information. It is imperative that we reconsider our pace through life and intentionally choose to slow down and, as Scripture puts it, "be still." Revival is not possible without the willingness to unplug from your hustle and your "busy." You need to stop and be still to hear God's voice. There is no other way. When it comes to rethinking my hustle, I wish I could be a little more like Martin Luther, who once said, "I have so much to do today that I shall spend the first three hours in prayer."

I owe much of this chapter to the thoughts and insights of John Mark Comer and his book, *The Ruthless Elimination of Hurry*, in which he implores us to rethink our "hurry" and slow down our lives to the pace of Jesus. I love how he has not only caused me to stop and rethink my hustle but also to pause and rethink what the "wilderness" means to me.

For a very long time, I saw this wilderness as a place of chastisement and a place that I was very keen to see the back of. Maybe, like me, you, too, have been eager to close your desert chapter and move on to revival and the Promised Land. The Greek word used in the New Testament for wilderness is *erémos*, which can also be translated as a solitary, desolate, lonely, or a needed quiet place. John Mark highlights that Jesus regularly returned to the *erémos* to pray and seek silence and solitude. We read in the Gospel:

"Very early in the morning, while it was still dark, Jesus got up, left the house and went off to a solitary place (erémos), where he prayed." - Mark 1:35

"But Jesus often withdrew to lonely places (erémos) and prayed." – Luke 5:16

Oh, come on! Are you serious? Do we need to regularly and ungrudgingly come back to the wilderness? We have just spent thirty-nine days trying to figure out how to get out of this desert, and now they are saying we need to return constantly and eagerly. Well...that's what Jesus did. Who are we to argue?

The reason is that Jesus knows we need to slow down and be still. We need a quiet place. We need a place of silence and solitude where we can regularly find time for reflection, reaffirmation, repentance, and revival. We need the desert.

In a world that has become so quick, where we are frantically moving from commitment to responsibility to obligation, how can we slow down? In a life that is so rushed and where hurry is the norm, what are we to do? With our minds and thoughts running at a hundred miles an hour, what is the prescribed course to follow?

Do you just keep going quicker and quicker, or do you choose to listen to and remember the count, Quick, Quick, Slow..., Slow..., Quick, Quick, Slow... Slow...

As life gets busier, we tend to neglect our time in the *erémos*, our quiet place. We too easily give in to the time-consuming machine we call life. Ironically, it is during these busy times that we most need to go slow. That is how Jesus modeled His ministry: the busier He got and the more demands there were on His time, the more He protected and cherished His quiet time in the *erémos*. Though counterintuitive it is essential.

Jesus not only modeled this practice. He instructed his disciples to do the same, and if we are truly his disciples, then that includes us:

> *The apostles returned to Jesus and told him all they had done and taught. And he said to them, "Come away by yourselves to a desolate place and rest a while." For many were coming and going, and they had no leisure even to eat. And they went away in the boat to a desolate place (erémos) by themselves.* – Mark 6:30-32(ESV)

As our lives become busier and our minds become more hurried, we should

- Come away
- By yourself
- To a desolate place, and
- Rest a while

We don't need more podcasts or Bible studies. We need to be still, and we need to be intentional in slowing down. This will look different for each of us, but what is important is to find silence and solitude regularly. We can't control the quick pace of the world around us, nor can we reign in the number of thoughts bombarding us throughout the day... but we can choose to be still and remember to count to the dance of life...

Quick, Quick, Slow... Slow... Quick, Quick, Slow..., Slow....

The *erémos* is calling you... How will you respond? Or are you too busy being busy?

Day 40: **No Filter!**

Rethinking MY MESSAGE?

Humor is often a wonderful comfort when we are going through a difficult desert season. We've all met someone who, even with ominous clouds hanging over them, can make the situation lighter with a joke. My wife will often remind me that being funny is not one of my talents, but regrettably, that has never deterred me from trying.

A few weeks after her surgery to remove the brain tumor, we sat in the doctor's gloomy office. As he discussed her prognosis and what we could expect going forward, the little bit of hope that we had mustered up post-surgery quickly evaporated. He did not sugarcoat anything, Glioblastoma... Stage IV... Life expectancy was sixteen months at best... Limited treatment options... no current clinical trials... The more he spoke, the quieter we became.

He explained that the tumor had been removed from the left frontal lobe and, as a result, we could expect to see changes in how she reacted to emotional and strenuous circumstances. As he kindly phrased it, she might have "less of a filter" when trying to express herself. I answered quickly and sarcastically, saying, "Oh, don't worry, doctor; She has never really had a filter." Fortunately, they both appreciated my sense of humor in that moment, and we could all enjoy a good laugh together.

As we were about to leave his office, Brenda turned to him and kicked straight into her "no-filter" mode, "Doctor, I appreciate that you're smart and know your stuff, but you are wrong... Just so you know, I am not a statistic, and I refuse to become one... I will beat this!" He smiled, saying, "I believe you."

Filters are good; they keep our engines clean, they purify the air in our homes, and they keep the coffee grinds out of our morning cup of java. Having a filter that stops you from verbalizing every thought that comes to your mind is a useful attribute and well-advised. But we may be doing more harm than good when we try to filter the Gospel message to make it more "acceptable." The underlying question is: Why do we find it necessary to filter the Good News? Does it need tailoring, or do we do this to protect ourselves from prejudice or backlash?

Only you can share your story and the impact of the Gospel on it. Our time in the desert is part of our testimony, and we are called to rethink our message. For much of my life, I have felt the nudge to testify and share the Gospel, but most of the time, I have quickly talked myself out of it. What if I say something wrong? Maybe I should wait until I am better equipped. Get another degree, or listen to a few more podcasts. What if I offend someone and push them completely away? What if I don't have the answers? Maybe I should wait until God has answered all my prayers and delivered me before I start to witness. Filters, that is what these questions were, and in the end, they simply hindered the spirit from using my testimony.

The book of Exodus tells us the story of how Moses led the Israelites from captivity and slavery in Egypt into the wilderness en route to the Promised Land. But things had not exactly panned out as they had hoped for, and they found themselves stuck in this desert. During this time, Moses' father-in-law,

Jethro, comes to visit him in the desert. We need to take note that Jethro was not a Jew but a Midian priest. We read:

> *Jethro, Moses' father-in-law...came to him in the wilderness... Moses told his father-in-law about everything the Lord had done to Pharaoh and the Egyptians for Israel's sake and about all the hardships they had met along the way and how the Lord had saved them.*
> – Exodus 18:5,8 (NIV)

I find this interaction between Moses and Jethro quite intriguing. Jethro comes to Moses while he is still in the wilderness. He is nowhere near the land that he had been promised and seems to be stuck in the middle of a desert season. I am certain that he had doubts, questions, and ample reason not to share his testimony. God had yet to deliver them. He was in a barren waiting period. Nonetheless, he tells of God's great deeds amid his trials.

Moses drops the filters and shares about God's providence in his "story-in-progress" despite Jethro's different faith. Note that it is not about preaching good doctrine or religion but just about telling the unfiltered truth of what God has already done and what He is still doing. Moses does not edit out the hard bits but highlights how God continues to save them in the desert. He doesn't censor the truth to appease his audience or remove the difficult unanswered parts.

Moses' testimony highlights two principles: there is no need to postpone nor filter the message. Jethro's response below should cause us all to stop and rethink our message:

> *He said, 'Praise be to the Lord, who rescued you from the hand of the Egyptians and of Pharaoh, and who rescued the people from the hand of the Egyptians. Now I know that the Lord is greater than all other gods, for he did this to those who had treated Israel arrogantly.'*
> – Exodus 18:10-11 (NIV)

Moses did not wait until he arrived in the Promised Land before he started ministering and testifying. In the same way, we should not wait until all our prayers have been answered to tell what God is already doing. We have reason to testify while we wait in the desert. Also, being real about our current struggles and trials is more important than having all the answers, and people will respond to this. By rethinking our message and rendering our hearts, we find revival, even if this revival looks a little different from what we set out to find. Maybe revival is about bringing your father-in-law, your friend, your child, or even your pastor to Christ by testifying of the great things He is doing while you are wandering in the desert.

As I write the last words in this book, I _reflect_ on my journey through the wilderness, and I confess that I don't have all the answers yet. The future remains uncertain, and I don't know what tomorrow will look like. There are days when I'm barely holding on and days when my failures and shortcomings lead me to a dark valley. But I look up and _reaffirm_ what I know to be the truth. God has never left or forsaken me; He carries me through the valleys. I am moved to praise as I look back and see His hand in everything. Though I stumble and fall, I see how He loves me, and I am compelled to _repent_ because of His overwhelming love. I know that I am free, and the shackles are broken. My mind is renewed, and my heart is rendered to His will. I have found _revival_. I have not just survived this wilderness...but I am alive and kickin' or should I rather say... I am revived and kickin'.

This is my unfiltered testimony. It is not pretty, not perfect, but it is real and still a work in progress. My prayer is that as you turn the final page, you, too, can echo Jethro's response to Moses' testimony... "Now I know that the Lord is greater than all other gods."

Not The End.... The Beginning.

About the Author

Joel de Jesus was born and raised in South Africa. He qualified and registered as a Chartered Accountant and started a career in auditing, financial management, and business. He was a successful entrepreneur before deciding to immigrate with his young family to the United States.

His American dream soon became a nightmare as he experienced setback after setback. In addition to the challenge of moving a young family across the globe, he also had to face business and financial failure, job loss, self-deportation and struggles with depression and self-harm. But this was just the beginning, as he soon found himself navigating the uncertain life path once his wife was diagnosed with a life-threatening GBM brain tumor.

In his struggles, he felt God's calling to prepare for life in ministry and duly enrolled to study an MDIV at the Reformed University. He graduated with honors and as valedictorian in 2024.

He currently serves on the Board of Directors for a local church and is also involved with leading middle-school students.

Joel is a die-hard Liverpool FC fan and spends his free time watching and following them. He loves hiking and supporting local performing arts.

Learn more about Joel de Jesus: https://revivedandkickin.com/